Confl &
Cooperation

Rochdale and the Pioneering Spirit
1 7 9 0 - 1 8 4 4

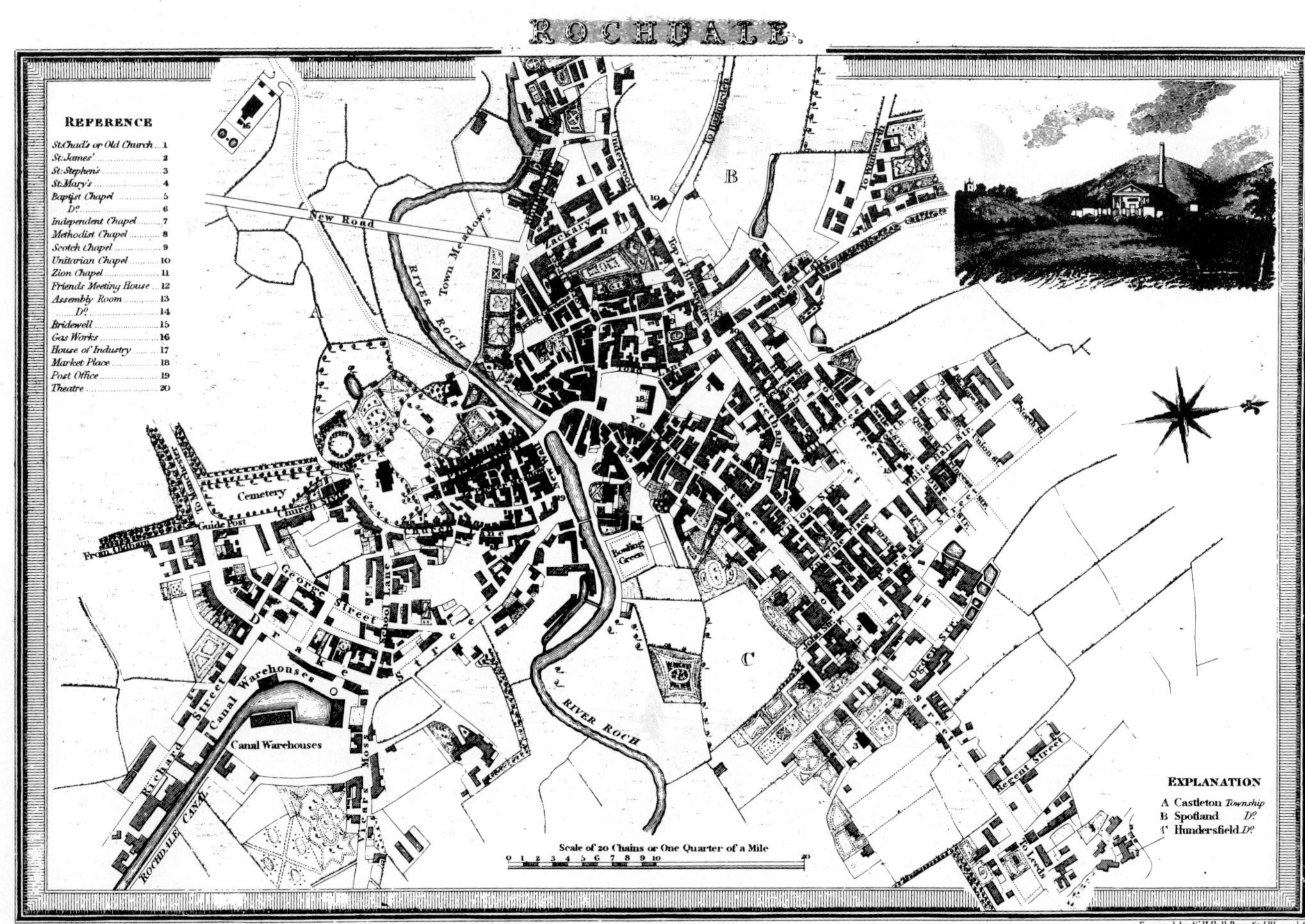

Rochdale in 1824

Conflict & Cooperation

John Cole

George Kelsall
Littleborough
1994

This is for Sue

ISBN 0 946571 24 4

Published by George Kelsall, The Bookshop,
22 Church Street, Littleborough, Lancashire
OL15 9AA. Telephone 0706 370244.

Printed by RAP Ltd, 201 Spotland Road,
Rochdale OL12 7AF.
Telephone 0706 44981

Contents

Acknowledgements

To Dorothy Thompson, lifelong radical and the outstanding modern historian of the Chartist movement, my sincere thanks for the generous and flattering foreword.

Thanks also to Anita Teuton for her faultless typing, to Sue for the proofreading and to Pam Godman, Joy Hopwood and the staff at Rochdale Local Studies Library for their patience, help and suggestions.

Thank you Roger Baldry, Assistant Director Rochdale MBC Recreation and Community Services for permission to reproduce the illustrations from the same excellent Local Studies Library.

Thank you, of course, to publisher George Kelsall and finally to Neville Kirk of Manchester Metropolitan University for his support and encouragement over the years.

Foreword by Dorothy Thompson

Rochdale people have good reason to be proud of the fact that theirs was the town in which modern Co-operative trading finally got off the ground as an efficient and profitable enterprise. The movement which started here formed an essential part of the British labour movement for a century and a half as well as giving inspiration and guidance to similar movements throughout the world. Few people in Britain with some interest in history are unaware of the story of the pioneers and the famous institution in Toad Lane. But for many people in the 1990s few things are more boring than the Co-op and all that goes with it in the way of dusty and predictably-laden shelves and stores which represent all that is old-fashioned and un-trendy in the world of retailing.

The old-style Co-op may well be a thing of the past, but the ideals and methods of Co-operation are in fact being revived today in many unlikely places. In the United States various forms of co-operative retailing have opened channels for the delivery of good fresh agricultural produce to town dwellers in defiance of the trends in supermarket shopping. In towns and cities in Europe numerous systems of joint purchase and of mutual financial support are being developed among people for whom access to large-scale credit is impossible. The needs of the small buyer for good quality necessities and for a reasonable degree of choice have led many to devise fairer and more egalitarian ways of conducting commercial transactions of all kinds, in spite of the power and privilege of the massive and dominant concerns.

John Cole's account of Rochdale is therefore of interest not only to historians and to Rochdale local patriots. By showing how the ordinary men and women of one town tackled a range of problems created by technological change and the weight of free-market ideology amongst the politically and industrially powerful of the time, issues are raised which transcend the purely local or strictly chronological. In this compulsively readable account of a key period in the history of Rochdale, we can see the way in which a variety of forms and institutions arose by which people attempted to control their own destinies, to protect their living and working conditions and to combine adaptation to the new with respect for traditional institutions and attitudes. By showing the previous political and industrial experience of the first pioneers, this study demonstrates the climate of ideas in which the early Co-operative movement was born. In some essential matters they established practises - such as the recognition of the property rights of married women and the democratic voting rights of members — which were outside, indeed against, the existing laws of the country, and which were only attained nationally after many years of campaigning.

Historians will welcome the use of hitherto unpublished documentary and local press material, and the arguments presented here will feed in to a number of ongoing controversies. But the account is above all one which helps to restore the idea of human agency and choice to the history of the society and economy of one town in a period of disturbance and change. It is a success story in many important ways, and may perhaps go some way to offer an antidote to the general gloom of a society in the midst of a major depression.

Dorothy Thompson, 1993

Dorothy Thompson is the author of numerous books and articles including *The Chartists* (1984) and *Queen Victoria, Gender and Power* (1990).

Rochdale and Cooperation: a brief chronology

1750 and following. Growth of nonconformity in the Rochdale area.

1760 and following. Gradual mechanization of local textile industry.

1760. First English Co-operative founded by the dockers of Chatham and Woolwich.

1771. Birth of Robert Owen, the prophet of Co-operation.

1783. First Sunday school founded in Rochdale. Thousands of working people provided with elementary education.

1791. First factory chimney in the town of Rochdale.

1795. Bread riots in Rochdale, at least one fatality.

1808. "Shuttle Gathering" riots in the town. Barracks established.

1817. Politically motivated march of the "Blanketeers" from Manchester to London includes a large Rochdale contingent.

1817. Political protest meeting at Cronkeyshaw, Rochdale.

1819. The Peterloo Massacre.

1824. Repeal of the Combination Acts. Rochdale Journeymen Weavers' Association founded. A list of wages is agreed by The Association and local manufacturers.

1825. Police Commission — the forerunner of Rochdale Council — established.

1827. Weavers strike successfully over wage levels.

1827. Weavers launch partially successful campaign against "Truck Shops".

1828. William King of Brighton founds the influential journal, "The Co-operator."

1828. Weavers fail to prevent the introduction of mechanised spinning processes into Healey Dell Mill.

1829. Riots in Rochdale following weavers' strike. Union Secretary deported for life.

1830. Weavers' strike unsuccessfully supported by John Doherty's National Association for the Protection of Labour.

1832. Parliamentary Reform Act. Whig/Liberal John Fenton defeats the "people's candidate" James Taylor — the minister of Clover Street (The Co-operators') Chapel.

1833. Short-lived "Owenite" Co-operative store opened at 15 Toad Lane, Rochdale.

1835. Radical, later Chartist, leader Feargus O'Connor visits Rochdale. Radical Association founded with James Taylor as President and Thomas Livsey as Treasurer.

1835. Parliamentary Election. Radicals split the vote allowing Tory John Entwistle to be elected M.P. for Rochdale.

1837. Anti-Poor Law demonstrations in town led by Thomas Livsey.

1838. Establishment of Socialists'. Institute in Rochdale. Venue used by Chartists, Owenites and Trades Unionists, Thomas Livsey Treasurer.

1839. Female Radical Association founded.

1839. Local agitation for total abolition of compulsory Church Rate payment.

1839. Chartist Thomas Livsey becomes Police Commissioner (councillor).

1839. Major Chartist activity in Rochdale. Arms freely available in Rochdale market. Drilling on the moors.

1840. Church Rate dispute divides Parish.

1840. Chartist James Leach becomes Mayor of Rochdale.

1841. Parliamentary election. Ultra-radical William Sharmon Crawford elected M.P. for Rochdale.

1841. Major economic distress in the area.

1841. Chartists discuss the opening of a Co-operative Store.

1842. Plug Plot Riots. Strikes paralyse the North-West. Local strikers call for implementation of the Charter.

1842. Plans for Co-operative store in the town reported in the Manchester Guardian.

1844. Weavers' strike. Meetings in the Socialists' Institute and elsewhere result in plans for opening a store. Shop finally opened by "Rochdale Pioneers" in December at 31 Toad Lane, Rochdale.

1849. Collapse of Rochdale Savings Bank ensures success of Pioneers' venture.

Introduction

Co-operation with a capital "C" is about working together according to mutually agreed principles. It places power in the hands of ordinary people and provides educational opportunities, employment and a way of life for millions. It proposes an alternative economic system to capitalism and has well over 700 million adherents worldwide.

Co-operative organisations include, amongst others, consumer societies, thrift and credit societies and agricultural, housing and womens' productive societies.

Co-operative principles, Co-operative production and Co-operative trading thrive in the unlikeliest of places. Huge in Japan, big in South America, throughout Europe,Asia and behind what was the Iron Curtain, the Co-operative ethos acknowledges no geographical boundaries.

What binds these different organisations together is not a common religion, culture or language but a set of principles — principles devised by ordinary working people in Rochdale, Lancashire. The Rochdale Principles, as they became known, are based on the concepts of democratic control, equity in membership and education — a solid base to be sure — but why did these principles born out of a particular set of circumstances in a comparatively small Northern town become the accepted standards of a worldwide movement?

The answer lies in the unique combination of common sense and idealism contained in the Principles — a combination which both parallels and reflects the development of the working class in the Rochdale area. Rapid industrialisation resulted in hunger, poverty, disease, social dislocation and widespread unrest. In a series of increasingly co-ordinated activities, ordinary people working collectively evoked responses to these changing conditions. In the process, they developed their own organisations, institutions and societies. One such society was that of the Rochdale Equitable Pioneers, the originators of the Rochdale Principles who, in opening a small shop at 33 Toad Lane in December 1844, gave birth to the modern Co-operative Movement.

Historian E.J. Hobsbawm, in discussing the concept of self-organisation during the early Industrial Revolution, made the following observations. "Self-organisation", he said, was visible:

> *in the local Primitive Methodist Community ... in the dense concentration of Workers' Mutual and Friendly Societies in the new industrial areas, especially in Lancashire, but above all in the serried thousands of men, women and children who streamed with torches on to the moors for Chartist demonstrations and in the rapidity with which the new Rochdale Co-operative shops spread in the late 1840's.*[1]

It is this concept of self-organisation which provides the key to explaining Rochdale's legacy as the birthplace of Modern Co-operation.

The town was once described as the "clearing house for ideas"[2] between Lancashire and Yorkshire and certainly its geographical situation made it a natural stopping off place over many centuries for both traders and travellers. From the late eighteenth century, mail coaches would halt at the old Roebuck Hotel on Yorkshire Street, dropping off newspapers, pamphlets and journals to a population as hungry for news and ideas as they often were for bread.

Ideas and theories were avidly discussed in the town's pubs and clubs — some were quickly discarded, others were taken on board, yet others were adapted to suit local needs.

Gradually, over a period of about fifty years, local people learned to work together and organise for their own benefit, channelling energies originally expended in unco-ordinated protests into sustained demands for human rights and drawing from their experiences in self-organised institutions such as Friendly Societies, trades unions and nonconformist chapels.

Co-operation was merely one of the many responses by local people to the massive social problems caused by industrialisation. Both industrialisation and the economic system which was developing with it — industrial capitalism — were new phenomena and just as there were no precedents or guidelines for people to follow, there was no guarantee that either system was necessarily here to stay. It was therefore the particular genius of working people that they devised mechanisms for their own survival in what was a period of unprecedented change and uncertainty.

In the following chapters we shall look at collective action and leadership in churches and chapels, in trades unions, in the demand for the vote (Chartism), in local and Parliamentary elections and finally in Co-operation. What we shall see will include riots and uprisings, drilling and armed demonstrations, attacks on mills and factories, cruelty, scandal and corruption but above all the triumph of hope over adversity and the effectiveness of self-organisation.

1. From Market to Mill Town

St. Chad's Church, "the spiritual centre of one of the largest parishes in the country"

Rochdale's geographical location on the border with Lancashire and Yorkshire meant that its industrial and social development was influenced as much by events on the Yorkshire side of the Pennines as by happenings in Lancashire. As a result, it remained a woollen producing town until well into the nineteenth century.

A route from Halifax to Rochdale over the bleak, inhospitable crags of Blackstone Edge predates written records and there is ample evidence on the hills of the presence of Bronze Age hunter-gatherers. Maybe the Romans used a routeway across Blackstone Edge, nobody knows for sure, but certainly the town is mentioned (as Recedham) in the Domesday Survey of 1086 and the Parish Church of St. Chad probably predates the first known appointment of a vicar (in 1194) by at least two centuries.

The town is therefore of far greater antiquity than most settlements in industrial Lancashire and it was as the spiritual centre of one of the largest parishes in the country that the town grew in importance. A market charter was granted in 1251 and the small hamlet on the Roch became a commercial centre for the farmers scattered over the eleven square miles of windswept moorland which constituted the Parish of Rochdale.

Gradually, this "hardy mountain breed" began to augment their meagre income by keeping sheep and the local woollen industry was begun by smallholders and farmer weavers who plied their trade unaffected by the Guild restrictions in force in large corporate towns such as Preston.

Because of their isolation, farmer weavers became more and more reliant upon middlemen to either supply the raw materials or to sell on the partially completed goods. The pubs which grew up around the market doubled up as exchange houses and on market days inns such as the Bishop Blaize (named after the patron saint of woolcombers), the Woolpack and the Market Tavern were crammed with merchants, weavers and wheeler-dealers. By the mid-seventeenth century, virtually every ginnel and alleyway around Blackwater and Lord Street supported at least one place of refreshment for the thirsty traders of the Parish.

In the 1750's, just prior to the dawning of the Industrial Revolution, the staple manufacture of the Rochdale area was "a branch of the woollen trade consisting chiefly of baizes, flannels, kerseys, coatings and cloths" produced mainly for export. In Oldham, Bolton and Blackburn, by way of contrast, a cloth with a linen warp (the vertical thread) and a cotton weft (the horizontal thread) was being produced. These areas became the early cotton centres whilst Rochdale, which developed into the national centre for plain-weave flannel, did not become a cotton producing area until much later. Indeed, it was not until the 1830's that cotton superseded wool as the town's major industry. So as well as being of a greater age than many of the surrounding towns, Rochdale's industrial evolution was significantly different, being in some ways a hybrid of developments in Lancashire and Yorkshire.

The "putters-out", the middlemen, eventually transformed themselves into merchants, establishing trading links with Europe — especially Portugal — and even the New World. Some, but not all, were of Puritan stock and, as we shall see, nonconformists of a bewildering number of persuasions came to flourish in the area. As early as the seventeenth century, these merchant clothiers began to invest in the land and to replace their modest wooden houses and halls with imposing stone-built structures. The Holts of Ashworth, the Butterworths and Chadwicks erected these monuments to the Glory of God and Mammon, for themselves and for their descendants.

Dynasties rose and fell as sons and grandsons became more landed gentry than merchants, lost interest in the family trade and fell upon hard times. Meanwhile in the tiny cottages clinging to the hills, life went on unaffected by these fluctuations in fortune:

> *Farms were mostly cultivated for the production of milk, butter and cheese ... The farming was generally of that kind which was soonest and most easily performed and it was done by the husband and other males of the family whilst the wife and daughter attended to the churning, cheesemaking and household work and when that was finished they busied themselves in carding, slubbing and spinning the wool as well as forming it into warps for the loom. The husband and sons would next... size the warp, dry it and beam it in the loom and then they, or the females would weave the warp down.*[1]

And in all winds and weathers the raw materials, the woven cloth, general supplies of all kinds, lime, sandstone, everything that could be, was loaded on to the backs of tiny Galloway ponies and tortuously conveyed over the treacherous packhorse routes to markets near and far, at home and abroad.

Even industrialisation, when it finally arrived, was slow and painful. Kay's Flying Shuttle was not generally adopted, even in the cotton areas, until the 1760's and the inventions of Arkwright, Hargreaves and Crompton were not adapted to the flannel industry until much later.

Up until this time, such factories as existed were water powered, often former corn mills, restricting early industry to the plentiful Pennine streams and rivers. Along the valleys of Naden, Cheesden and Deeply, as well as amongst the densely wooded slopes of Healey Dell, the ghostly remains of the first generation of textile mills are still clearly visible.

While the rivers and streams outside the town had already been curdled and coloured by dyes and oils, Rochdale itself remained, until the 1780's, virtually unaffected by the taint of industry. Of course, by then it had grown into a market town of some prosperity but there were, as yet, no factory chimneys.

Domestic Woolspinning in 1775: by John Collier (Tim Bobbin)

"Rochdale remained almost untainted by industry until the 1780's" . . .
Rochdale Town Centre c.1750

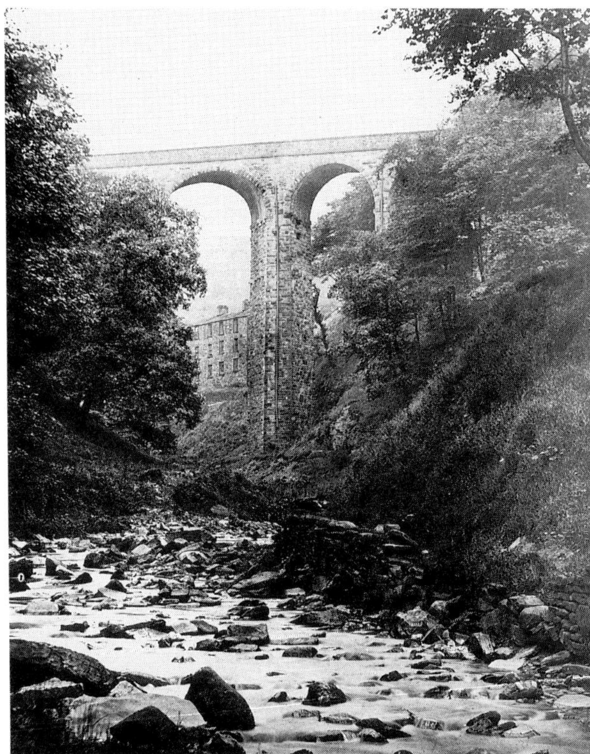

The early industrial Valley at Healey Dell

The Smiths, merchants with important trading connections with Portugal, had already built a town house which later became the Duke of Wellington Hotel, the market had been removed from outside the Parish Church to an area at the bottom of Yorkshire Street and the Vavasours had built what is today Lloyd's Bank as their town residence. They had also created a passageway, which they named the Walk, to connect their stylish home to the riverbank; the Roch itself still flowed through the centre of the town under the one bridge linking South Parade to the grassy area known as the Butts. Just below, the river was forded and standing at the edge of the ford looking up towards what is now Drake Street, townsfolk would have seen the then familiar sight of the windmill adjacent to Summercastle House.

The first factory chimney in the town when it appeared, in or around 1791 on Hanging Road, was a major attraction. The novelty soon wore off! With the arrival of the factories in the town, came the weavers' cottages. Not all textile processes were mechanized simultaneously, weaving being the last sector of both the woollen and cotton industries to move into the mills. As, therefore, there was a rapidly accelerating demand for those skilled in weaving, hundreds of small master manufacturers moved from the rural areas to the towns where they built, or had built for them, special weavers' cottages with loomshops on the third floor. There, they employed journeymen, paid on piece rates, to weave the carded wool into flannel.

These three storey weavers' cottages appeared not only in the growing textile villages such as Littleborough, Milnrow and Wardle, but also in the then undeveloped areas of Rochdale such as Drake Street and the wide open spaces of upper Yorkshire Street.

Steam power transformed the town and mechanised industry pauperised the weavers. To contemporaries it seemed as though Rochdale had changed virtually overnight. Within a decade of the first factory chimney being built, the town was choking on smoke and filth. Thousands of farmer weavers abandoned their meagre living on the harsh Pennine hills to seek employment in the mills and factories and as the birth-rate grew, a spectacular increase in population produced overcrowding and conditions of barely imaginable filth

"Speculative builders threw up hovels" ... Greenwood's Yard

and squalor. Speculative builders threw up hovels as closely packed as possible and fit only for the pigs kept by the wretched poor.

As cotton superseded wool and factory processes replaced human labour, the handloom weavers were gradually reduced to starvation level. Unfortunately, because the pace of industrial development meant that this did not happen in a single year, or even during a single decade, there was never the incentive for weavers to leave the industry en-masse. Instead, handloom weavers suffered a slow and painful decline from the early 1820's to the late 1840's.

Neither was it just the weavers who suffered. The general standard of living during the same period was little better. To give some idea of the rate of growth of the town: the number of inhabitants rose from around 14,000 in 1801 to 23,000 a mere twenty years later. By 1841 the population was a staggering 68,000.[2]

As this rapid increase would probably suggest, Rochdale was a town largely composed of working class people. Of the 68,000 inhabitants in 1841 only 4% could be defined as professional people, "gentlemen", landed proprietors or clergy and only 13% were employed in traditional crafts or trades such as joinery, carpentry or smithing. The overwhelming majority of working people (44%) were employed in textiles whilst 10% worked in other factories and 8% were labourers. And yet all the power was concentrated into the hands of that 4% who constituted the town's élite.[3]

To sum up, therefore, Rochdale in the second decade of the nineteenth century, was a well established, but rapidly expanding town with a unique pattern of industrial development (which was creating a growing number of increasingly impoverished domestic workers.) As we shall see, until the early 1830's it had a ruling elite which was only fitfully interested in governing the town, and a growing manufacturing class who desperately wanted to govern but were legally prevented from doing so. It was also home to tens of thousands of increasingly bitter working people with no stake in the system whatsoever, beyond a miserably inadequate wage and a leaking roof over their heads which was not theirs to mend.

Who, then, did govern the town and Parish of Rochdale? As we have seen, the cottages of the farmer-weavers were scattered over one of the largest parishes in the country. For the purpose of what passed for local government in the 1820's, the Parish was divided into townships — Spotland, Wuerdle and Wardle, Blatchinworth and Calderbrook, Castleton and Butterworth. The town of Rochdale lay within the boundaries of four of these townships and had no independent powers of local government. Not until 1825 was an attempt made to create an administrative structure for the town itself. Traditionally, therefore, the only real power lay with the Church of England clergy and those members of the rich mercantile families with any ambitions to govern. One pointer to the future, however, was the long-standing tradition of Township Meetings which were called to ratify decisions made by the local élite and which were virutally open to all.

Nevertheless, as far as authority was concerned, the Parish Church of St. Chad was the heavenly body around

James Griffith Dearden, Lord of the Manor of Rochdale in the 1860s

which the town's Tory gentry revolved and the vicars of Rochdale, when they condescended to actually live in the Parish, were figures of considerable power and influence.

The Manor boundary coincided with that of the Parish and in 1822 the Manor rights were purchased by James Dearden from the poet Byron. Dearden energetically set about establishing a dynasty and single-mindedly blocked any attempt at reform which affected himself, his family, his status or his property. However, despite the fact that the Manor Court Leet of Rochdale still met, Dearden's power was more imagined than real.

Much of the genuine power that the Anglican Tory gentry wielded came from their legal monopoly of the

Kelsall and Kemps giant mill complex in the centre of Rochdale — Henry Kelsall began his working life with four looms and a jenny

magisterial bench. Intermarried merchant families such as the Royds and the Entwisles, together with the vicars of the Parish, therefore had total control of the local legal machinery. The petition sent to Central Government in 1825 for the creation of a Police Commission was an attempt to extend the powers of this small, restricted group into a single local government system for the whole of the town of Rochdale.

This attempt, however, was to be forcibly challenged. Although not all the new millowners and manufacturers were nonconformists (and therefore, by definition almost, opponents of the Anglican Tories), many were. And those who *were* nonconformist identified themselves politically as Whigs and later as Liberals. Some called themselves reformers because they favoured a gradual reform of the system in order that they may wield power themselves; because although many of this group had become wealthy, they had not yet become politically powerful. They could not vote and they were prevented by their religion from becoming magistrates.

Many of this wealthy fraternity were self-made men, with a burning ambition to succeed.Two examples will suffice: Henry Kelsall, the founder of Kelsall and Kemp's flannel empire began his working life with four looms and a jenny in the insalubrious and run-down Packer Street area, whilst John Chadwick was an innkeeper, also in Packer Street, before establishing himself as a woollen manufacturer and one of the largest employers in Rochdale.

As factory based industry took off, money poured in. The Kelsalls, the Chadwicks, the Brights, the Heapes and the Howards all prospered beyond anyone's, bar maybe their own, wildest dreams.

The fact, therefore, that they were unable to vote in Parliamentary elections caused them immense frustration and bitterness. However, from 1825 onwards they were entitled, as substantial ratepayers, to sit on the new Police Commission, and it was here, the early equivalent of the town council, that they first challenged the monopoly of power enjoyed by the Tories.

In order for their challenge to succeed, however, this numerically small middle class initially needed the support, the sheer weight of numbers, of Rochdale's increasingly angry and unpredictable workforce. Once these energies had been successfully utilised and the Whig/Liberal middle class had won their local power struggle, the same workforce would then have to be controlled and subdued. In Rochdale, as we shall see, this was to be no easy task — ordinary people also wanted a stake in the system.

2. Churches and Chapels

West Street Baptist Chapel

One of the first tastes of self-organisation that ordinary people experienced was provided by nonconformist chapels. Religion was important in nineteenth century politics, not because everyone attended church or chapel regularly (at a rough estimate only 30% of manual workers in Rochdale in 1851 were churchgoers), but because, especially in the Rochdale area, religious affiliations so clearly equated with political allegiances.[1]

Although there were obviously exceptions, the chances were, that in the 1850's, say, if you were a regular member of the congregation of St. Chad's Parish Church, you had Tory sympathies, if you were a member of the Baillie Street United Methodist Free Church, you were a "reformist" Whig/Liberal and if you attended either the Clover Street Unitarian Chapel or the Primitive Methodist Chapel, your politics were "left-wing" or what was known as radical.

This is borne out by the Church and Chapel registers of the period which reveal the middle class congregation of the Baillie Street Chapel compared to the overwhelming number of textile workers and labourers attending the Smith Street Primitive Methodist Chapel and the equally grass-roots congregation of the "Co-operators' Chapel" — the Unitarian Church on Clover Street.[2]

Historian G.D.H. Cole doubted if any town of Rochdale's size "was equally prolific in religious controversies and foundations. New churches and chapels were continually being formed and among the dissenting (nonconformist) congregation there were constant shifts and secessions and foundations of new sects".[3]

The first split from the Church of England in Rochdale occurred in 1688 when the former Vicar, Robert Bath, founded a Unitarian chapel in the town. Wesleyan Methodism took off in the mid-1750's, the Baptists established their first chapel in 1773, the Methodist Unitarians split from the Wesleyans in 1808 and in the same year the Society of Friends (Quakers)

St. Stephen's Countess of Huntingdon's Connexion Church

opened their Meeting House near the top of Yorkshire Street. Then came the Particular Baptists, the Countess of Huntingdon's Connexion, the Swedenborgians, the Independents and ... scores of others. In a survey taken in 1717 there were no Roman Catholics in the town, then, with the digging of the Rochdale Canal and the import of Irish labour, came the establishment of St. John's Church in 1829.

And this was just in the town! In the rural areas it seemed as though virtually every cottage, farmhouse, shippon or barn doubled up as a place of worship, or equally importantly as a meeting place for ordinary people.

Much of this diversity was a result of increasing friction between the classes. Again, as G.D.H. Cole noted, "No point of Wesley's (John Wesley the founder of Methodism) teaching took stronger hold than that which made it part of man's duty to God to achieve success in his calling".[4] This was interpreted by many millowners as the justification to accumulate enormous wealth and, as a direct result, the intolerence and drive of many early Wesleyans alienated large numbers of Christian working people. Driven, therefore, from the larger churches and chapels, many people sought refuge in the tiny meeting rooms which sprung up throughout the area.

Meanwhile the middle class — the millowners and manufacturers — established other churches and chapels at their own expense; huge, imposing structures such as the Baillie Street United Methodist Free Church, which contained more pews than would ever be needed — even in a far more religious age than our own.

The major loser, numerically at least, in this religious revolution was undoubtedly the Anglican Church — the Church of England. In 1750 the Church of England could claim nearly 75% of regular churchgoers, declining to 30% of the total by 1843.[5] One of the major effects of tis decline was the growing opposition to the payment of a tax, payable by all ratepayers in the Parish, whether Anglican or not, for the upkeep of St. Chad's Parish Church.

From the mid-1820's on, this principle was challenged by nonconformists of all denominations, together with some members of the Church of England who felt that a compulsory tax or rate was fundamentally unjust and in 1839, when the political temperature generally was rising, there was a movement for total abolition.

Under considerable pressure, the vicar of the day agreed to a poll or ballot which he originally declared open for five days, hurriedly extending it to six when it became obvious that the opposition was in the lead. Despite the Church eventually winning that battle, the call for the abolition of the Rate became even more vocal. When a second ballot organised by a new vicar, the Rev. J.E.N. Molesworth, went in favour of the anti-Rate faction, the vicar virtually ignored the result and called yet another ballot.

Feelings were now running so high, with opponents organising protest meetings throughout the parish, attending noisy rallies both inside and outside St. Chad's and parading the streets, that the *Manchester Guardian* reported: "Another poll will endanger the peace of the town."[6]

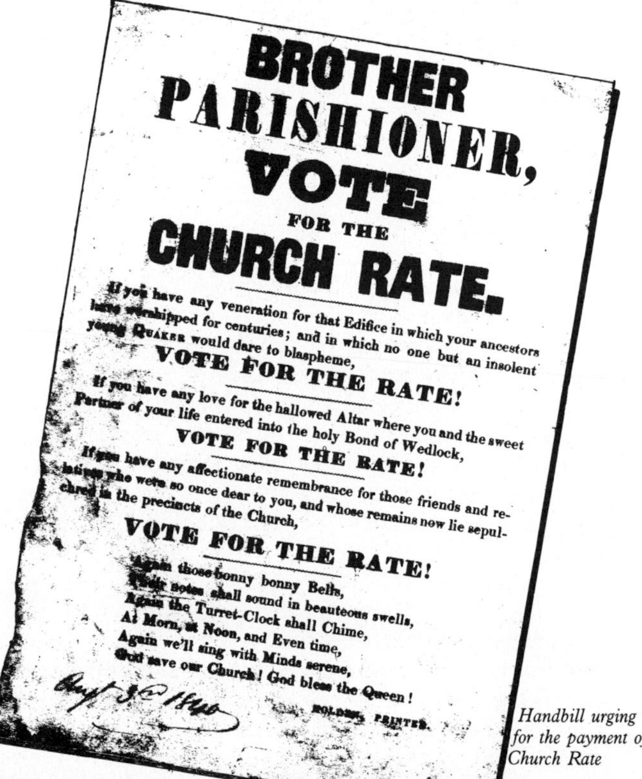

Handbill urging support for the payment of the Church Rate

The anti-Rate party, led now by radical and Chartist Thomas Livsey (of whom we will hear much more) threw their propaganda machine into top gear. One story was circulated that bailiffs, ordered to repossess some item of property in lieu of the rate, "took a poor man's Bible and sold it to obtain money"[7] and another that young women were being sacked from their jobs, "because their fathers and brothers would not vote at the Churchwardens' bidding."[8]

THE RATCHDAW
CLOWN;
OR, THE
GENIUS BRIGHT.

TUNE.---JINGLING JOHNNY.

A Cotton Spinner of great renown,
Attended a meeting in his native town,
As a public man he had long wish'd to pass,
But was by their VERDICT considered an Ass.
This man of smooth-face and straight-cut-coat,
Mounted a Tomb-stone and thus he spoke :—
Says he to keep a Church we never go in,
I won't, and don't you, fork out any tin.
But the Church from the State, I quickly will sever,
And we won't grant a Rate, *no not* never ;
The Tyrants to take twopence halfpenny a year,
From a poor oppress'd people, 'tis too much to bear.
Listen and silence, be mindful, I spake it ;
A man had a Bible and these fellows did take it,
But a time is at hand when for your relief,
Houses thatch'd with pancakes and built with roast beef,
Shall to your astonishment truly appear,
And the Heav'ns in kindness will shower out Beer ;
The Corn Bill we've got and we never will yield,
Until by our efforts this Bill is repeal'd,
When at the corner of every street there will meet ye,
A fat sucking pig, crying "come eat me, come eat me."
O John, friend John, of mem'ry BRIGHT,
Under a bushel hide thy light,
And ne'er again in any Town,
Show to the folks the RATCHDAW CLOWN.

Query :—Friend John, if thou "never discharg'd a Workman" for voting against thee, didst thou ever discharge a Tradesman ?

8th Mo. 5th, 40.

S. Ashworth, Printer, Rochdale.

Poster satirising John Bright's part in the Church Rate dispute

These incidents, according to the *Manchester Guardian*, "inflamed the working classes almost to a state of madness".[9] Middle class non-conformists were equally inflamed and mad. John Bright (the son of a local millowner who was to become a member of the Liberal Cabinet), addressed a huge and excited meeting in the churchyard. Balanced on a gravestone, supported by Thomas Livsey, Bright hurled abuse at the vicar and churchwardens to the mingled cheers and boos of the assembled multitude.

The actual poll was complete mayhem. "Free drinks and refreshments of all kinds were liberally distributed for those who would vote for the Rate"[10] and in one incident John Bright's brother Thomas was propelled into the church and up to the altar, borne aloft by the upraised arms of hundreds of excited parishioners. The militia was called out by the Tory magistrates then dismissed by the Liberal magistrates and a narrow victory for the vicar and the pro-Rate party had the whole parish in turmoil.

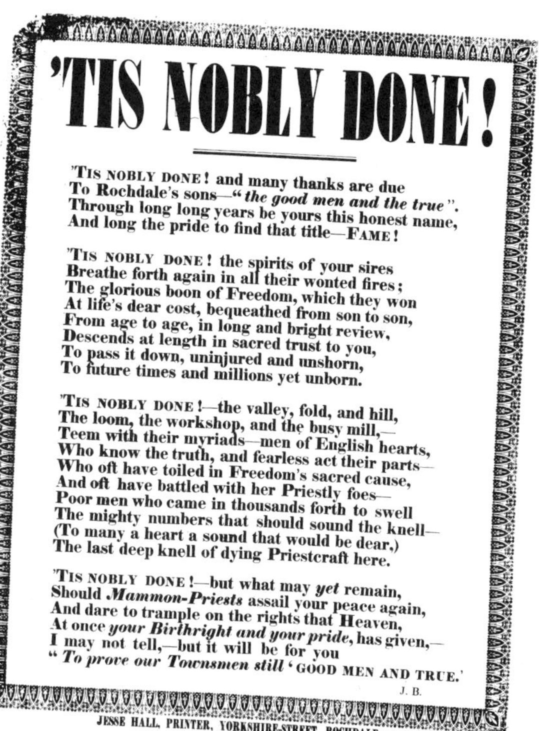

'TIS NOBLY DONE!

'TIS NOBLY DONE! and many thanks are due
To Rochdale's sons—"*the good men and the true*".
Through long long years be yours this honest name,
And long the pride to find that title—FAME!

'TIS NOBLY DONE! the spirits of your sires
Breathe forth again in all their wonted fires;
The glorious boon of Freedom, which they won
At life's dear cost, bequeathed from son to son,
From age to age, in long and bright review,
Descends at length in sacred trust to you,
To pass it down, uninjured and unshorn,
To future times and millions yet unborn.

'TIS NOBLY DONE!—the valley, fold, and hill,
The loom, the workshop, and the busy mill,—
Teem with their myriads—men of English hearts,
Who know the truth, and fearless act their parts—
Who oft have toiled in Freedom's sacred cause,
And oft have battled with her Priestly foes—
Poor men who came in thousands forth to swell
The mighty numbers that should sound the knell—
(To many a heart a sound that would be dear,)
The last deep knell of dying Priestcraft here.

'TIS NOBLY DONE!—but what may *yet* remain,
Should *Mammon-Priests* assail your peace again,
And dare to trample on the rights that Heaven,
At once *your Birthright and your pride*, has given,—
I may not tell,—but it will be for you
"*To prove our Townsmen still* 'GOOD MEN AND TRUE.'

J. B.

JESSE HALL, PRINTER, YORKSHIRE-STREET, ROCHDALE.

John Bright's triumphant response to the final outcome of the Church Rate dispute

Eventually, after both the pro and anti-Rate factions had began publishing magazines to promote their causes, a system of voluntary collection was established locally and the issue was resolved at national level in 1867.

During the agitation the working classes had received confirmation (if any was necessary) of the power and effectiveness of working collectively, together with the pressures which could be exerted by sheer weight of numbers.

Other lessons were being learned inside the churches and chapels — because it was here, or rather in the Sunday schools, that ordinary people were first taught the "three R's".

The first successful Sunday school in Rochdale was founded in 1783 by James Hamilton in White Beaver Yard. The school was supposedly inter-denominational but, even in the early years, a strong Methodist influence resulted in an affiliation with the Union Street Methodist Chapel. Although not an independent working class institution, the school found in printer James Hartley a champion of self-help and mass education. Under Hartley's leadership the school prospered and by 26 October 1806, the minute book reveals that within the school there were:

Girls who write 80
Girls in the testament (reading) 150
Girls in the spelling and alphabet 514
Boys who write 80
Boys in the testament 100
Boys in the spelling and alphabet 312[11]

It was even resolved that no preaching should take place at lesson time and the open nature of the school in 1814 is revealed by an entry in the minute book to the effect that: "books should be provided for those whose parents were so poor that they could not be found by them".[12] Teaching began at 10 o'clock in the morning until 12 midday and continued from 1 o'clock until 3:30.

Unfortunately, if the experiences of one Robert Standring, is anything to go by, the teaching methods employed by the schools in the 1820's were primitive to say the least.

St. James Church and Sunday School in rural Ashworth

> *I was only ten when I began to teach boys older than myself. I was expected to thrash them as well as to teach them and although the timid were overawed, the resolute were hardened. I have seen boys, for very trifling offences set on a form in the middle of the school, a Bible being placed in their hand which they were forced to hold as high as possible for 5 minutes ... I have once seen the holy book thrown down furiously to the ground by a boy who was punished in this way and at another time a boy was being punished for one little thing or another when his sufferings enraged him so much that he drew a large clasp knife with which he threatened to stab any teacher who would threaten him again.*[13]

Despite such negative experiences, until the 1840's, Sunday schools provided the only meaningful education for vast numbers of working people. After that period the middle class dominated Wesleyan Conference actively discouraged the teaching of the "three R's" in favour of a much narrower religious education. Literacy, it was felt, was a dangerous weapon in the wrong hands.

Nevertheless, thousands of working people had already learned much from their religious upbringing, particularly in the self-organised chapels and meeting houses. Many had become literate; many had also learned how to organise and delegate responsibility and Rochdale, with its unparalleled variety of denominations and sects, became a centre for radical nonconformity.

Two concepts — class and camp meetings — evolved in local chapels were introduced into the Chartist Movement in the 1840's. The class meetings divided the organisation into small cells for discussion, debate and decision making whilst camp meetings brought thousands of people together in the open air to listen to invited speakers and to ratify decisions. Both concepts were borrowed from Methodism and both spread from Rochdale to Lancashire and Yorkshire and then nationwide.

3. Bread Riots and Shuttle Gathering

Prior to the Industrial Revolution the "Common People", it was tacitly agreed, had natural rights under the law of the land which, if they did not provide wealth or advancement, at least ensured a kind of rough justice. The nobility, it was held, had a responsibility to look after the broad and general interests of peasants and the labouring poor — a responsibility recognised (within certain limits) by the nobility themselves.

In times of high food prices, the poor would frequently resort to riot or "unlawful behaviour". Such action was considered a safety valve and was a signal to the ruling class that a problem existed under this undefined natural law. Often, the distribution of food or a temporary adjustment of prices, would alleviate the situation.

The Industrial Revolution changed all that. As towns expanded and industrial capitalism took off, there were no longer any easy solutions. The unspoken bond between "master and man" was broken and the poor could no longer rely on the wealthier members of society to provide for them in time of need. Working people became "factory hands", food riots took on a more sinister aspect and protest became more focused and more political.

In the late eighteenth century, Rochdale experienced two major bread riots but it is significant that the second, in 1795, lingered in the memory of local people, not only because of the death of two of the participants, but equally because of the high profile of local vicar and magistrate Thomas Drake (as in Drake Street) who had called in the militia.

In 1795 a dearth of bread there was
and people cried for bread
The chiefest shepherd of the flock
(Drake) he feedeth them with lead
The people standing on the bridge
and thinking of no harm
It was then they shot old Bob
i'th'ead and wounded him i'th'arm.
Old Fletcher he was killed also as
you should understand
He was a farmer very good in tilling
of the land.
Now the old men are dead and gone
and must this world forsake
And all this evil it was done for the
quacking of a Drake.[1]

There followed a period of industrial unrest caused in some areas by the introduction of machinery and, in parts of the North-West, by falling wages in the domestic cotton and woollen industries. In 1808 there were a series of disturbances throughout Lancashire following the rejection by the government of the proposal for a minimum wage. In Rochdale, angry woollen weavers broke into the loomships (weavers' cottages) and removed the shuttles. Several were arrested and a large number of shuttles recovered by the authorities were taken to the small jail or "lock-up" on Rope Street. Further incensed by this action, an angry crowd marched to the jail, released the prisoners and burnt the building to the ground. The incident was reported in the *Times* of 7 June 1808.

A number of weavers have been compelled to leave their looms and have been deprived of their shuttles by the mal-contents, rewards for their apprehension have been offered by the magistrates: the cavalry are scouring the country and general alarm prevails. The small gaol at Rochdale ... has been burnt down

> *by them and a few of their incarcerated brethren liberated. A respectable manufacturer at Haywood (sic) was dragged from his bed last night and severely beaten by a party of weavers.*[2]

So volatile did the situation become in Rochdale, that the magistrates (including, still, the Rev. Dr. Drake) called in the Halifax militia who "marched from Halifax to Rochdale in a drenching rain"[3] and remained for a whole day and night before returning home.

As a direct result of these disturbances Rochdale became a barracks town with a permanent military presence on constant alert for any threat of unrest or rebellion.

By the second decade of the nineteenth century, influenced very much by the democratic movements in America and France and particularly by the concepts of "Liberty, Equality and Fraternity", local protests had become more politically orientated. The Reform Movement, as its name implies, demanded a reform of the existing parliamentary system with its restricted voting rights, under-representation of the new industrial towns and its "Rotten Boroughs".

Following the march of the Blanketeers (so called because these demonstrators carried sleeping blankets with them on their protest march from Manchester to London), the first political reform meeting in the country was held on Cronkeyshaw Common, Rochdale. Middleton radical Sam Bamford recalled that "the town wore an appearance of alarm and a company or two of soldiers were under arms in the main street".[4] A handbill, distributed throughout the town, announced that the meeting was called:

> *To take into consideration the most speedy and effective way by which the laws of nature and the ancient constitution of our country furnish us with, to obtain a reform on the Principles of Universal Suffrage, annual Parliaments and election by ballot.*[5]

The call for Universal Suffrage (the vote for all), annual elections and a secret ballot or vote was adopted in the late 1830's by the Chartist movement. But even in the second decade of the century, many working people believed that their conditions would only improve if they had a say in the governing of the country. The meeting on Cronkeyshaw Common, or more particularly the procession which preceeded it, caused great excitement in the town:

> *The procession began to move about 2 o'clock and was headed by at least 5000 female reformers and followed by about 30,000 men bearing but too sad an evidence of the distress of the times, but withal so terrible in their appearance as to make the boldest tremble ... The cap of liberty was carried in front with other banners bearing inscriptions: on one was "Destruction to all legitimate governments", on another "Annual Parliaments etc. or death to those in authority who oppose their adoption", on a third "The memory of Paine, Brandreth etc." and on a fourth "Success to Female Societies".*[6]

The active participation of women in protest movements continued throughout the period we are looking at with "female societies" a constant factor during times of heightened political activity. Women maintained a high profile in the Chartist camp meetings and in demonstrations and processions, virtually leading the Chartist revival single-handed in the area in 1848. What our male dominated history does not tell us, however, are the *names* of more than a handful of the hundreds of female political activists.

Back in 1817, the female-led procession had yet to reach Cronkeyshaw when a drunken bystander shouted the less than popular phrase "Church and King!" causing, according to a correspondent to the Manchester press:

> *such a scene of terror and I may add mischief as never before occurred in this place. What windows were left exposed were shattered in an instant.*[7]

Two years later, there occurred the incident at St. Peter's Field, Manchester which was forever referred to afterwards either simply as Peterloo or more commonly as the Peterloo Massacre. Thousands of local protestors,many of them handloom weavers, led by Sam Bamford, streamed into Manchester to what was planned to be a peaceful demonstration for Parliamentary Reform. When, following the orders of magistrate the Rev. Hay, the cavalry opened fire and, in the ensuing panic eleven demonstrators were killed and over 400 seriously injured, there was almost universal horror and condemnation.

Manchester

OR LITERARY, COMMERCIAL,

Price 7d. Ready Money. 8s. per Quarter in Credit.

SATURDAY,

No. 32.

Manchester
PUBLIC MEETING.

A REQUISITION having been presented to the Boroughreeve and Constables of Manchester, signed by above 700 Inhabitant Householders in a few hours, requesting them to call a PUBLIC MEETING "To consider the propriety of adopting the most LEGAL and EFFECTUAL means of obtaining a REFORM in the Commons House of Parliament" and they having declined to call such Meeting therefore the undersigned Requisitionists give NOTICE that a Public Meeting will be held, on the area, near St. Peter's Church, for the above mentioned purpose, on Monday the 16th instant—the Chair to be taken by H. Hunt, Esq. at 12 o'clock.

* Major Cartwright—Mr. Wooller—Mr. Pearson—Mr. Carlisle—Dr. Crompton—Edward Rushton—Mr. J. Smith—Mr Thomas Smith—will be invited to attend this Meeting.

Manchester, 6th August, 1819.

Enoch Shaw, 15 Tassle-alley
Daniel Johnson, Pendleton
George Bramhall, 18 Back-ballon-street
John Melling, 130 Deansgate
Benjamin Rushton, 12 Sutcliff-buildings
Joseph Hindley, Rogers-row
Edward Medcalf, 22 do.
Joseph Wood, 32 Sackville-street
Thomas Edleston, 21 China-lane
Thomas Clarke, 17 Waterloo-street
Andrew Clark, 28 Cumbeland-street
John Austin, 37 Turner-street
Samuel Green, 10 Ark-street
James Addenson, Oaythorn-street
David Wilson, 4 Colliers-row
Samuel Wetherel, 19 Brierley street
John White, Moreley-street
George Ramscan, Back-hanover-street
John Nuttal, Worsely-street
William Shawcroft, 8 Bradley-street
Patrick Fay, 4 Back-mather-street
Thomas Johnson, 6 Mart-street
Edward Clarck, 8 Peter-street
Derby Bryne, 11 Cooper's place

Contemporary newspaper advertising the meeting at St. Peter's Field, Manchester. 7 August 1819

Significantly, Rochdale millowner and Liberal Thomas Chadwick, who had witnessed the events, described the incident as "an inhuman outrage committed on an unarmed, peaceful assembly".[8] This experience had a profound and lasting effect on Chadwick who, together with his brother, William, were probably amongst the most sympathetic to the working class of all the "reformist" middle-class millowners. So much so, that in the 1840's William Chadwick, by then himself a magistrate, refused to use the militia as a means of crowd control.

In 1819, by way of contrast, stunned disbelief greeted the appointment as the new Vicar of Rochdale of the man who had ordered in the troops at Peterloo — the Rev. Dr. Hay.

The 1820's, as we shall see, were years of increased trades union activity in Rochdale, again largely involving handloom weavers, but in the early 1830's there was another concerted effort to extend voting rights.

The "Peterloo Massacre"

Throughout the country, an irresistible tide of opinion forced the government to consider at least some measure of Parliamentary reform. During the agitation leading to the passing of what became the 1832 Parliamentary Reform Act, the wealthy but voteless middle classes sought and received the support of those further down the social ladder. In this way, protests became mass protests and demonstrations became popular demonstrations.

By way of example, in May 1831, a public meeting was held in the Butts, Rochdale:

> *Henry Kelsall, the High Constable, presided ... There were at least*

6,000 inhabitants present, chiefly of the working class ... The speakers were all manufacturers and tradesmen and as they entered most cordially into the feelings and distress of their poorer neighbours, they were loudly cheered.[9]

When the Reform Bill eventually became law, a triumphant procession was organised by the town worthies. Down Drake Street behind the Chief Constable (mayor), the Vicar, the Lord of the Manor and the millowners and manufacturers (now able to vote), marched "The firemen, the lamplighters, the traders, the smiths, the Friendly Ironmongers and the letterpress printers", the vast majority of whom, in common with the thousands who lined the route cheering, were excluded from voting under the Act.

The result of working class disillusion, when this became clear to all, was a lasting sense of bitterness and betrayal. However, once again the power of public protest and mass organisation had been demonstrated.

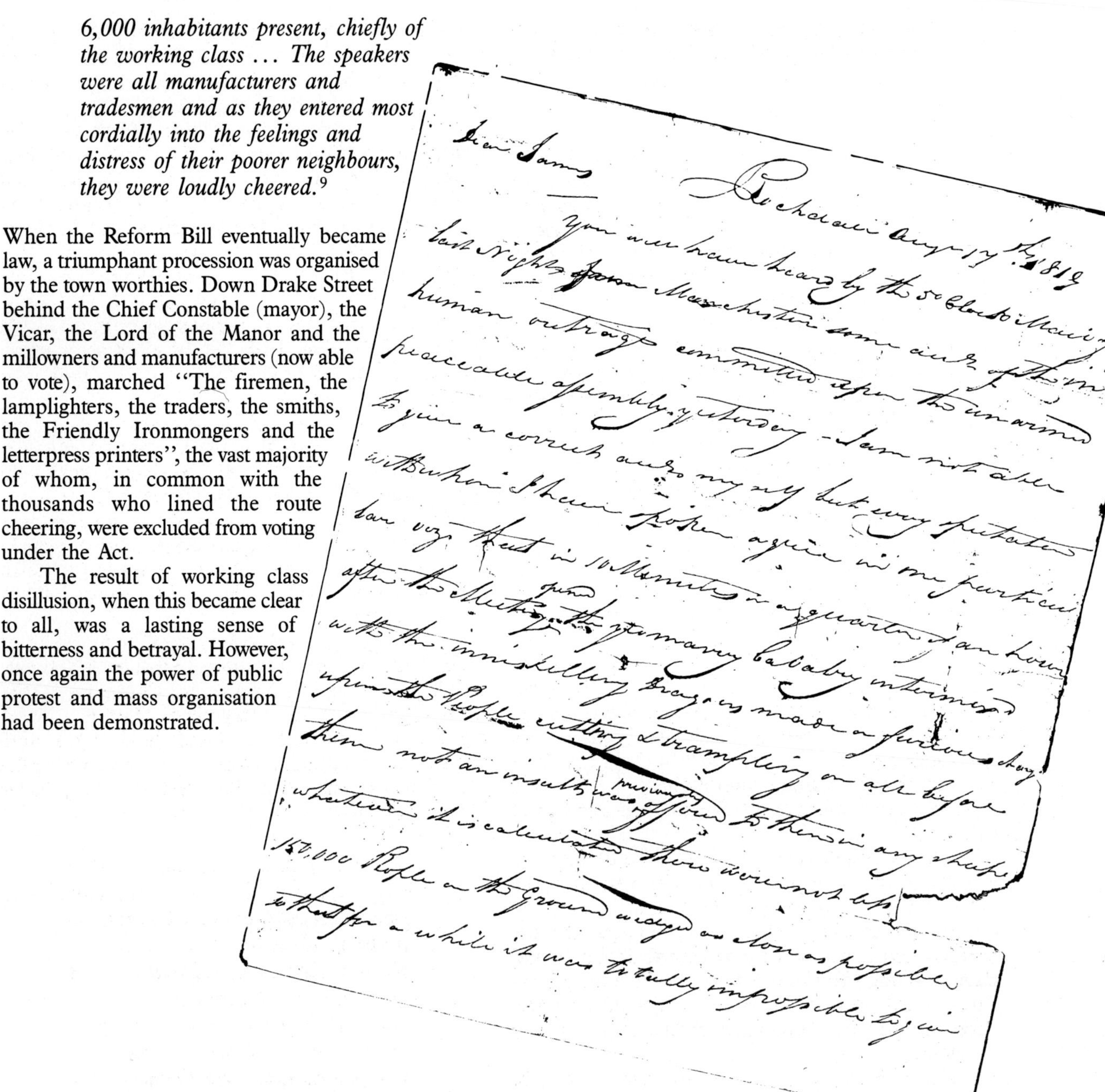

Dear James

Rochdale Augt 17th 1819

You will have heard by the 5 o'clock Mail of last Nights from Manchester some acct of the inhuman outrage committed upon the unarmed peaceable assembly yesterday - I am not able to give a correct acct of my own but every spectator with whom I have spoken agree in one particular viz. That in 10 Minutes or a quarter of an hour after the Meeting opened the yeomanry Cavalry intermixed with the Inniskilling Dragoons made a furious charge upon the People cutting & trampling on all before them not an insult was previously offered to them in any shape whatever it is calculated there were not less 150,000 People on the Ground wedged as close as possible so that for a while it was totally impossible to gain

Extract from Thomas Chadwick's eyewitness account of Peterloo

4. Midnight Mischief

In the early nineteenth century, no aspect of life remained unaffected by the rapid changes brought about by industrialisation. People lived increasingly in shabby cities, towns or industrial villages. Domestic industry was declining whilst the factory owners imposed a disciplined regime on the workforce, unknown in an earlier age. No wonder then, that one of the earliest forms of self-organisation was centred around work.

Trades and Craft Guilds had existed since the Middle Ages but it was with the coming of industry that trades unions began having a major impact on local affairs. The Rochdale area was particularly important in the first phase of nineteenth century trades unionism and experiments in organisation within the local handweaving sector were widely imitated.

Initially, local weavers were most concerned with protecting their status. Weaving, although undoubtedly a craft, was not a prohibitively difficult skill to acquire and as the century progressed, there was a huge influx of outside labour into the trade, leading to attempts by well-established weavers to block entry and restrict apprenticeship. By the late 1820's, however, local weaving unions became almost exclusively concerned with attempting to halt the decline in their standard of living.

Four issues were of major concern.The first of these was the continuing problem of incomers into the industry, the second was the reduction in employment caused by the introduction of machinery into the factories and the third was the growth of Truck and Badger shops (Truck shops were where employers "paid" staff in food and goods, rather than money; Badger shops offered unlimited credit at crippling rates of interest).

The fourth issue was that of the rate for the job. Weavers wages were standardised by custom and practise and long-term security was sought via wage lists jointly agreed between weavers and masters. There were, in effect, piece rates with weavers paid a standard amount for a certain length of finished cloth.

Officially, trades unions were illegal from the passing of the Combination Acts in 1801 until their repeal in 1824. However, in order to establish and monitor the agreed wage lists, both weavers and manufacturers had their own combinations or unions. Both sides had some interests in common (the flourishing of local trade for example) and both sides had weapons to employ if negotiation broke down. Although not based in a single factory, weavers could resort to the rolling strike, whilst employers simply locked weavers out of the workplace and blacklisted identified troublemakers.

Interestingly, in Rochdale, the weavers had another, rather surprising weapon — public sympathy. As their conditions declined, and as long as their protests were not considered "extreme", the "Weavers Committee" was frequently able to take advantage of some measure of public support. The Committee was also extremely adept at propaganda and publicity, releasing a stream of handbills and posters, often to the great discomfort of their employers.

A fascinating insight into this "illegal" period of local trades unionism is provided by that most notorious incident in early trades union history — the transportation of the Tolpuddle Martyrs. These agricultural labourers from Tolpuddle in Dorset were transported to Australia, at least in part, for copying the initiation ceremony of the Rochdale weavers. A letter to the *Leeds Mercury* revealed:

> *how the mode of initiation was the same as practised years before by the flannel weavers of Rochdale with a party of whom the thing, in the shape it then went, originated ... A great part of the ceremony, particularly the death scene, was taken from one division of the Oddfellows who were flannel weavers in Rochdale.*[1]

TO THE JOURNEYMEN
WOOLLEN
WEAVERS
Of the Parish of Rochdale.

FELLOW LABOURERS,

THE Committee of Journeymen Woollen Weavers of this Parish, deeply impressed with a sense of the importance and necessity of an UNION, upon a firm and liberal basis, between all the Journeymen Woollen Weavers of this Parish, are desirous that the same may be communicated to every individual Journeyman Woollen Weaver, who is now in Society, or whom Societies may think proper to receive.—Considering that UNION in itself is so essential, not only to the peace, but also to the prosperity of any Community or Society.—The principle of UNION has the sanction also of Divine Authority, being inculcated in the sacred pages of HOLY WRIT: it is there said, "can two walk together except they be agreed." and as, by walking together, we must understand all the transactions and connections of Men, (both civil and religious) in their social intercourse one with another; and, if Unity is so essential to the peace and good understanding of two only, how much more so to ten, twenty, a Society, Community, or a Nation!!!

Brethren, while the principal Inhabitants and Trades of the Nation are uniting and exerting all their power and influence in the establishment of various Institutions, for the avowed purpose of promoting the peace, prosperity, and happiness of the People, shall we, as a body, still be divided—shall we still continue to tear and devour one another, by WORKING AGAINST EACH OTHER TO THE INJURY OF THE WHOLE; shall we still continue to be wanderers in the land, as sheep having no shepherd, no control, no head, nothing to which we can refer, no place to which we can fly for shelter or security in time of peril or disaster, but still continue to expose ourselves to be torn, devoured, and annihilated by the wild ungovernable passions of PRIDE, MALICE, TYRANNY, and OPPRESSION; "tell it not in Gath, publish it not in the streets of Askelon," suffer it not to be said in the Nation, that, at a time like the present, when all that can be lawfully obtained is necessary, that the Journeymen Woollen Weavers refuse to be united.

But Brethren, there are some of you, whose timidity and apathy perhaps arise from a fear of the Combination Laws, as it is fresh in some of your memories, that several persons have been imprisoned under the power of those Laws, bnt the Legislative Powers in their Wisdom must have considered that UNION was necessary, and have therefore repealed the Combination Laws. You cannot now be consigned to a prison, for uniting in a peaceable and orderly manner, TO SUPPORT OR RAISE YOUR WAGES. Some of you, again, are taking a retrospective view of the late Institution—to these we must say, that one glance at our inward proceedings, would remove every donbt. You would find no *dissipated revelry*. No one assuming more authority than another. NO PAID OFFICERS. Our officers have hitherto given their labour, and borne their own expenses. Others are of opinion that our endeavours will prove fruitless!—to these,and to all, we must say that the fault rests not with us, but with you in not making an effort. Our cause is not hopeless, if you will come forward in a firm and persevering manner, bearing in mind that courage in the hour of danger is inestimable but when danger is over, courage is worthless.—WE ARE PERSUADED, THAT UNION WILL EFFECT EVERY PURPOSE.

Let us then, Brethren, entreat you to come forward without delay, recollecting (to quote the words of an able and experienced Statesman,) that "*Labour is the real Wealth of the Nation,*" *and in proportion as Labour is depressed and undervalued so must we droop and labour under difficulties.*

Should you be so fortunate as to accept this invitation, and join our Society—Generations yet unborn may have cause to bless our present efforts.

COMMITTEE:

James Smith, James Butterworth, Samuel Sharples, Edward Kershaw, James Tempest,
John Whitehead, John Turner, William Whitworth John Bamford, William Whitworth
Charles Kershaw, James Clegg, George Taylor, John Sladen, Edmund Howarth.

BRANCHES ESTABLISHED AT THE

FREE MASON'S ARMS, SCHOOL-LANE,
WOODMAN, - - - - - HIGH-STREET,
AMEN CORNER, - - - - LOWER-GATES,
WHITE LION, - - - - SPOTLAND.

N. B. Monthly Meetings held the second Saturday in each Month, at seven o'clock in the Evening. Persons to the number of seven, wishing to form Branches either in Town or Country, may meet with the necessary information, by applying to any of the afore-mentioned places, on the nights of meeting.

Committee Room, School-lane, Rochdale,
Sept. 26th, 1824.

T. WESTALL, PRINTER.

Recruitment poster for the Weaver's Union

A List of Wages agreed to be given by the undersigned Manufacturers.

Flannels.

PRIALS.

Reed	Weight (lb.)	£	s.	d.
18	42	0	18	0
	48	0	19	6
	54	1	1	0
19	42	0	19	0
	48	1	1	0
	54	1	2	0
20	42	1	0	0
	48	1	2	0
	54	1	4	0
21	42	1	1	0
	48	[illegible]	3	0
	54	1	5	0
22	42	1	3	0
	48	1	5	6
	54	1	7	9
	60	1	10	0
23	42	1	5	0
	48	1	7	6
	54	1	10	0
	57	1	11	3
	60	1	12	6
24	48	1	9	6
	54	1	12	0
	60	1	15	0
25	48	1	11	6
	54	1	14	6
	60	1	17	6

COUPLES.

Reed	Weight (lb.)	£	s.	d.
18	36	0	15	6
	38	0	16	3
	40	0	17	0
19	36	0	16	3
	38	0	17	0
	40	0	17	9
20	36	0	17	0
	38	0	17	9
	40	0	18	6
21	36	0	18	0
	38	0	18	9
	40	0	19	6
22	36	1	0	0
	38	1	1	0
	40	1	2	0
23	36	1	2	0
	38	1	3	0
	40	1	4	0
24	36	1	3	6
	38	1	4	6
	40	1	5	6
25	36	1	5	0
	38	1	6	0
	40	1	7	0
26	36	1	6	6
	38	1	7	6
	40	1	8	6

Reed	Weight (lb.)	£	s.	d.
27	36	1	9	6
	38	1	11	0
	40	1	12	0
28	36	1	13	6
	38	1	15	0
	40	1	16	6
29	36	1	16	6
	38	1	18	0
	40	1	19	6
30	36	2	0	0
	[illegible]	[illegible]	1	6
	40	2	3	0
31	36	2	5	0
	38	2	6	6
	40	2	8	0
32	36	2	9	6
	38	2	11	6
	40	2	13	6
33	36	2	10	6
	38	2	15	6
	40	2	17	6
34	36	2	17	6
	38	3	0	0
	40	3	2	6
36	36	3	11	0
	38	3	14	0
	40	3	17	0

YARD WIDES.

Reed	Weight (lb.)	£	s.	d.
20	44	1	0	0
	47	1	1	0
	50	1	2	0
21	44	1	1	0
	47	1	2	0
	50	1	3	0
22	44	1	3	6
	47	1	5	0
	50	1	6	6
23	44	1	5	6
	47	1	7	0
	50	1	8	6
24	44	1	7	0
	47	1	8	6
	50	1	10	0
25	44	1	8	6
	47	1	10	0
	50	1	11	6
26	44	1	10	6
	47	1	12	0
	50	1	13	6
27	44	1	14	0
	47	1	16	0
	50	1	17	6
28	44	1	19	0
	47	2	1	6
	50	2	3	6

Reed	Weight (lb.)	£	s.	d.
29	44	2	3	6
	47	2	6	0
	50	2	8	6
30	44	2	6	6
	47	2	9	0
	50	2	11	6

Drapery BAIZE.

Reed	Weight (lb.)	£	s.	d.
16	45	0	13	0
	51	0	15	0
	57	0	17	0
17	45	0	14	0
	51	0	15	9
	57	0	17	6
	63	0	19	0

Domett BAIZE.

Weight (lbs)	£	s	d.
30	0	13	6
36	0	15	0
42	0	16	6

Red Lists, Blue Lists, and Swan-skins.

PRIALS.

Reed	Weight (lb.)	£	s.	d.
18	45	0	16	0
	51	0	18	0
	57	1	[illegible]	0
	60	1	0	9
	63	1	1	6
19	45	0	17	0
	51	0	19	0
	57	1	1	0
	63	1	2	6

Reed	Weight (lb.)	£	s.	d.
20	45	0	18	6
	51	[illegible]	[illegible]	[illegible]
	57	[illegible]	[illegible]	[illegible]
	63	1	3	6
21	45	0	19	0
	51	1	1	0
	57	1	3	0
	63	1	4	6

COUPLES.

Reed	Weight (lb.)	£	s.	d.
18	[illegible]	0	15	6
	[illegible]	[illegible]	[illegible]	10
	[illegible]	[illegible]	[illegible]	[illegible]
	[illegible]	[illegible]	[illegible]	0
19	42	0	16	3
	48	0	17	6
	50	0	18	9
	54	0	19	9
20	42	0	17	0
	48	0	18	3
	50	0	19	6
	54	1	0	6
	58	1	1	6
	62	1	2	6
21	42	0	18	0

Reed	Weight (lb.)	£	s.	d.
21	46	0	19	4
	50	1	0	6
	54	1	1	6
	58	1	2	6
	62	1	3	6
	66	1	4	6
	70	1	5	6
22	50	1	2	0
	54	1	3	4
	58	1	4	6
	62	1	5	10
	66	1	7	2
	70	1	8	6
23	54	1	5	0
	58	1	6	6

Reed	Weight (lb)	£	s.	d.
23	62	1	8	0
	66	1	9	6
	70	1	11	0
24	58	1	8	6
	62	1	10	0
	66	1	11	6
	70	1	13	0
	74	1	14	6
25	58	1	10	6
	62	1	12	6
	66	1	14	6
	70	1	16	6
	74	1	17	6

Dometts.

Wool Carded and Spun for

PRIALS.

Reed	Weight (lb.)	£	s.	d.
18	30	0	15	0
	36	0	16	6
	42	0	18	0
19	30	0	16	0
	36	0	17	9
	42	0	19	0
20	30	0	17	0
	36	0	18	6
	42	1	0	0
21	30	0	18	0
	36	0	19	6
	42	1	1	0
22	30	0	19	6
	36	1	1	6

Reed	Weight (lb.)	£	s.	d.
22	42	1	3	6
23	30	1	0	6
	36	1	3	0
	42	1	5	6
24	30	1	1	6
	36	1	4	0
	42	1	6	6
	45	1	8	0
25	30	1	3	6
	36	1	6	0
	42	1	8	6
26	30	1	4	6
	36	1	7	0
	42	1	9	6

COUPLES.

Reed	Weight (lb.)	£	s.	d.
21	26	0	17	0
	28	0	18	0
	30	0	19	0
22	26	0	18	0
	28	0	19	0
	30	1	0	0
23	26	0	19	0
	28	1	0	0
	30	1	1	0
24	26	1	0	[illegible]
	28	1	1	0
	30	1	2	0
25	26	1	1	0
	28	1	2	6

Reed	Weight (lb.)	£	s.	d.
	30	1	4	0
26	26	1	2	6
	28	1	4	0
	30	1	5	6
27	26	1	4	0
	28	1	5	6
	30	1	7	0
28	26	1	5	6
	28	1	7	0
	30	1	8	6
29	26	1	6	6
	28	1	8	0
	30	1	9	6
30	26	1	8	0

Reed	Weight (lbs.)	£	s.	d.
	28	1	9	6
	30	1	11	0
31	26	1	9	6
	28	1	11	0
	30	1	12	6
32	26	1	11	0
	28	1	12	6
	30	1	14	0

The above are the Prices of Work in Stubbings, and any greater or less Weight to be paid for accordingly.——No Person to put his Work in a finer Reed than he is paid for.

J. & J. Fenton & Son
James Scholfield & Co.
Leach, Tweedale & Co.
Wm. Butterworth & Sons
George Ashworth & Co.
John Chadwick & Sons
Wm. Midgley & Sons
Thomas Howarth & Co.
Whittaker & Cross
James Barns & Sons
Hind, Dean & Co.
Turner & Whittle
Brearley & Lord

Joseph Mellor & Co.
W. & R. Turner
E. & R. Ogden & Co.
G. & J. Ashworth
John Howarth & Son
George Holt & Co.
Henry Kelsall
Robert Kelsall
Edward Ainsworth
Abraham Tweedale
Edward Clegg
Robert Crossley
William Scholfield

Edmund Lord
John Chadwick
John C. Scholfield
Robert Kay
Joseph Tempest
Benjamin Butterworth
Walter Fulton
William Robinson
John Scholfield
Jonathan Whitworth
Ralph Taylor
John Brierley
James Scholfield

John Lane
Thomas Clegg
William Roberts
John Kay
Abraham Brierley
John Howarth
Robert Healey
John Kershaw
Abraham Wood
James Charnock
Benjamin Scholfield

Rochdale, January [illegible]

HARTLEY, PRINTER.

The infamous Statement Price of 1824

In 1824 the Rochdale Journeyman Weavers Association, which represented both male and female weavers and jenny spinners, became legal and devised, in the opinion of the original historians of the trades union movement, "the best and simplest statement of aims of workers that the age had produced".[2]

By this time wage levels were dropping and the Association were able to persuade a number of major manufacturers to issue a joint statement:

> *The present low prices of labour in the manufacture of flannels is (sic) become a subject of vital importance to the prosperity of this parish. The first necessary step ... is to endeavour to equalise the present price of work by bringing up those who, from ignorance or any other motive have been giving less than the standard price of others.*[3]

In other words, the largest local manufacturers were prepared to put pressure on those of their colleagues who were threatening the stability of local trade by undercutting. (Undercutting had already caused a virtual collapse of the calico industry). The weavers, however, were not totally convinced that moral pressure would suffice and were collecting funds in anticipation of strike activity.

In the event, this did not prove necessary and the protracted negotiations resulted in what was known as the Statement Price of 1824, a jointly agreed and fiendishly complicated set of fixed payments for any given length of finished cloth. It is worth mentioning here that never, through all the traumas and turmoil which followed, did the weavers ever press for an increase in wages — the objective was always to maintain the rate of 1824.

The first breach in this agreement occurred only five months later, in December 1824. In a widely circulated handbill, the Association identified three major manufacturers — Richard Rostron, William Roberts and William Butterworth as the offenders but Rostron, in particular, had been undercutting for some time. The union, having solicited the support of the twelve largest manufacturers, called out Rostron's and Butterworth's weavers. After a twelve week strike during

Journeyman Flannel Weavers' Association Membership card

which the twelve "honourable" manufacturers demonstrated their support by employing the strikers, Rostron and Butterworth were forced to concede. Moreover, they were both persuaded to donate cash to the union's funds "as an encouragement to strike against other manufacturers who were paying lower than the Statement Price".[4]

When a government Select Committee investigating trades unions heard of the joint action of the Weavers' Association and the "honourable" manufacturers, they were appalled, describing it as: "a development, reprehensible and inconsistent with every practise of fair-dealing and justice".[5]

The following year saw a dreadful collapse in local living conditions which coincided with an attempt by manufacturers Brierley and Pilling to introduce a powerloom into their factory. The magistrates had received information, probably via one of the large numbers of government spies in the area, of a plan to burn the factory down. A crowd gathered on Tandle Hill with "an avowed intention of visiting the town"[6] and an eye witness reported that:

> *Colonel Byng has ordered a squadron of Hussars to march on the town. The crowd have not yet ventured to approach the town as we understand the factory (Messrs Brierley and Pillings) is to be defended and it will be necessary for them to carry firearms. As I write they have marched towards the factory intending for destruction.*[7]

Within hours, however, the crowd dispersed, having been informed of the imminent arrival of the troops. The Weavers Association swiftly denied any involvement with the proceedings:

PUBLIC
NOTICE
We, the present Committee of Management, b
longing to the WEAVERS' Union, understanding th
the Public are blaming us for attempting to fi
MESSRS. BRIERLEY and PILLING, Cotton Manufa
turers, of Rochdale, DO HEREBY DECLARE, th
whatever may be the state of the Case, we have n
Connection with it, neither do we intend to medd
with any thing but our own Trade.
By Order of the COMMITTE
J. WESTALL, PRINTER, 5, NEW-MARKET, ROCHDALE.

The Union denies any involvement in the attempt to burn down Brierley and Pilling's woollen mill.

> *We the Committee of Management belonging to the Weavers' Union understand that the public are blaming us for the attempt to fire Brierley and Pilling Cotton Manufacturers, do hereby declare that we have no connection with it.*[8]

NOTICE,
THAT THERE WILL BE A
PUBLIC MEETING
OF ALL
Woollen Weavers
AND SPINNERS,
Held opposite the HORSE SHOE, top of Blackwater Street, Rochdale, on Tuesday next, the 30th Instant, to ascertain how far the Weavers have succeeded in putting down the System of paying Wages in Provisions, and other Goods; and to make proper Arrangements for totally annihilating such demoralizing and degrading practices; and at the same time to ascertain how far the Manufacturers have reduced to practice the New Statement, and if found to be a reduction of Wages on the Statement of 1824, to remonstrate against it.
It is therefore the bounden Duty of all Weavers and Spinners, to come boldly forward and if any Grievances exist to state them, in order that Measures may be adopted to put a stop to all such illegal and unprincipled Practices.
THE CHAIR TO BE TAKEN AT 1 O'CLOCK.
By Order of the General Committee.
WESTALL, PRINTER, 5 -MARKET ROCHDALE.

The union's action against "Truck Shops"

Whatever the truth of that particular statement, there can be no denying the role of the union in the attempt to stamp out the Truck shops. In 1827 with the local economy still in decline, an increasing number of manufacturers adopted the practise of paying their workers in (high-priced) goods instead of cash. This issue was to gain prominence once again in the 1840's and was one of the factors which motivated the Rochdale Pioneers but in the 1820's, the Weavers' Association had considerable success in mobilising public sympathy. Even the local Tory newspaper, the *Rochdale Recorder*, was impressed by the campaign comparing "the present peaceful events" with "recent meetings which disgraced the good name of the working classes and which were called at the instigation of incendiaries".[9]

Several actions against the worst offenders were successfully prosecuted, funded by a "Robin Hood Club" which financed court hearings from the proceeds of previous convictions.[10]

The union's attempts to maintain the Statement Price of 1824 were, however, notably less successful. In March 1827, the effigies of two backsliding manufacturers were marched through the town and hung with all due ceremony from a gibbet. By then, very few manufacturers were paying the agreed piece rates and in desperation the union organised a general strike, gathering the shuttles from every loom shop and factory. Even during this period of heightened conflict, the weavers did not forfeit all public support and one correspondent to the *Rochdale Recorder* was convinced that the conflict would only be resolved "when the weavers fairly profit in the proceeds of the trade".[11]

The deadlock was eventually broken via the mediation of a local curate; the weavers returned the shuttles and a number of manufacturers agreed to reinstate the price agreement of 1824.

In the August of 1827, however, a dispute occurred which drove the final wedge between manufacturers and weavers. Two manufacturers, Henry Kelsall and Joseph Tempest, began producing a finished cloth of greater width than their competitors whilst paying the existing rates to their weavers. In calling for strike action the union declared that the weavers would only return to work if Kelsall and Tempest paid for any expenses (including strike pay) incurred during the stoppage.

A local magistrate announced that "he had never seen a more foul conspiracy against anyone."[12] Nevertheless, the Association continued to take the initiative. Henry Kelsall was one of the most successful and energetic of the new generation of Liberal "reforming" manufacturers. An ardent churchgoer, Kelsall was never slow to express his Christian concern of the plight of the working classes. When, therefore, the union in a widely distributed broadsheet proclaimed, "it is a proverb in our Sunday schools that the children whose parents have worked for Mr. Kelsall might easily be known for their ragged and meagre appearance", Kelsall capitulated, even agreeing to pay strike expenses of £367.[13]

Other manufacturers were furious, insisting that the union refund the money and restrict their activities to maintaining the 1824 Statement Price. Relations then broke down completely with the Association's attempt to block the introduction of new machinery into Leach and Tweedale's Healey Dell Mill. The union argued in a series of broadsheets that, "the setting aside of Spinning Jennies would throw hundreds of hands out of employ".[14]

This "interference" in the running of the mill was the final straw. "Who ought to govern?", thundered the *Rochdale Recorder* and, providing their own answer, "The masters undoubtedly!"[15]

The major manufacturers immediately bound themselves in a strike fund of £500 each in defence of Leach and Tweedale whilst the Association for its part solicited the support of local traders and where that was not forthcoming instructed their members:

> *Not to lay out money with any butchers, shopkeepers, publican, milkman, tailor, shoemaker etc. who refuses or neglects to contribute to our funds.*[16]

This was interpreted as intimidation by the manufacturers who loftily declared that they would "never support a union which seeks to support itself by falsehood, threats and midnight mischief".[17] After twelve weeks of total stoppage and with their strike funds finally exhausted, the weavers admitted defeat. In the ensuing negotiation they were forced to concede:

> *Never to interfere with mills and with improved machinery. Not to interfere in the regulation of handloom shops. To use no violence or intimidation in order to compel anyone to join the Association, nor to enforce the payment of expenses incurred during a strike against a manufacturer.*[18]

TERMS OF AGREEMENT MADE
BETWEEN THE
Woollen Manufacturers
AND
THE WEAVERS' UNION

THAT the Weavers' Union shall concede the Point in dispute, relative to its interference in Mills and with Improved Machinery;—and the Manufacturers engage, that any person employed to spin on an Improved Power Machine, shall be enabled to earn, on the average, as much as a Slubber can on a large Billy, which is, at the present, from 22*s*. to 24*s*. per Week.

That the Union shall not interfere in the Internal Regulation of Hand-Loom-Shops, further than as regards the payment of the Statement Price of Wages, of 1824; and, that it shall not interfere between any Manufacturer and the Makers in his employ.

That the Union shall be conducted on Free Principles, and no Intimidations, Threats or Violence, shall be used to compel, but, that any Lawful means may be taken to prevail on persons to join it;—and, that no Manufacturer shall object to any Weaver or Spinner, on account of his or her joining it.

That no Turn-out shall take place, or be supported by the Union, against any Manufacturer, before the particulars of the Grievance have been stated in writing to the Manufacturers' Secretary, at least one week before such intended Strike shall take place:—and further, the Union has no intention of enforcing the re-payment of any expenses incurred by a Strike against a Manufacturer, but, that any determination, relative to such Strike, shall be made by mutual consent of Manufacturers and Weavers.

In proof that the Union does not encourage any Intimidations or Threats, to be put in execution, in order to compel any person to comply in supporting it:—It offers £5, to be paid out of its fund, in conjunction with an equal sum from the Manufacturers, as a reward to those who will give information (so as to lead to conviction) against any individual or individuals, who shall, in future, commit violence on any one's person or property.

By order and on behalf of the Meeting of Manufacturers.

EDWARD CLEGG, Chairman.

Deputation of the Weavers' Union, with full authority to act on its behalf. ***John Crossley, James Buckley, Edward Clegg, Robert Lees.***

***Rochdale, March 4th,* 1828.** HARTLEY, PRINTER, ROCHDALE.

The Weavers' Union capitulates

So appalling were conditions now, with increased mechanisation and spiralling wages, that the weavers resorted to even more desperate measures. The events of 1828 and 1829 were played out on a rising tide of violence. "Midnight Mischief", as the manufacturers described it, included "Old Betty" (window smashing), machine breaking and exclusive dealing (only trading with those who supported the union).

In May 1829 the *Manchester Guardian* reported rioting in Rochdale, Blackburn, Manchester and elsewhere in Lancashire. In Rochdale "about twenty of the principal rioters were captured and taken to the New Bailey (the jail), an infuriated mob following. When the main body of the military left, the mob attacked the jail and, as the remaining troops opened fire, ten rioters were killed".[19]

During the subsequent trial of the ringleaders at the Lancaster Assizes, the aims of the rioters were revealed. Woollen manufacturer Thomas Robinson stated in evidence that:

> *At about six o'clock in the evening many hundreds of persons demanded that I should open the door of the loomshop. Before I could comply, they began to kick both myself and 8 constables who were on the premises. There were cries of "stone him" and "kill him" and a cry of "storm!" was repeated.*[20]

The crowd then broke down the door and smashed the rollers, spindles and spindle frames, incapacitating 24 looms.

Robinson, it transpired, was a target because he was hiring Knobstick (or blackleg) labour. Another factory which received the attentions of the machine breakers was that of William Chadwick, demonstrating that the new Liberal middle class were no more immune from the union's activities than their Tory counterparts.

Passing sentence on the defendants, the judge stated how he regretted seeing before him, "a number of men of industrious habits who had long contributed to support themselves and their families".[21] Thomas Kershaw, the secretary of the union and the identified ringleader, was made an example of and transported for life.

The weavers suffered a further (if temporary) blow and received another lesson in middle class indifference, or worse, when, at the height of the unrest of 1829, the Union's cashbox was stolen. Horrified by the calculated wave of destruction, several of the larger manufacturers had instructed a Parish Constable to hire Specials to guard their property. Following the assault on Thomas Robinson's factory, these Special Constables seized the Weavers' Union cashbox in the belief that it contained secret papers. The box was taken to the lock-up where it was opened and found to contain a large amount of cash but no documents, and locked again.

When the Constables later approached the manufacturers for payment "they point blank refused and suggested (it was alleged) that they should pay themselves out of the moneys contained in the weavers' chest''. Subsequently the Constables were seen ''to kick open the box and abstract the money''.[22]

William Woolley, one of the town's first deputy constables

Although those involved were later successfully prosecuted, the widespread belief that they had been encouraged in their actions by the manufacturers further soured both industrial and social relations.

By the beginning of 1830, weavers' wages had been reduced on average by 4s (20p) in the pound compared to the 1824 Statement Price. When James Schofield of Heybrook further reduced payments to 12s (60p) in the pound a large number of his fellow manufacturers followed suit, there was a general and complete strike of weavers throughout the district. On May 11th, according to the *Manchester Guardian*, there were ''six to seven thousand people thus out of employment''.[23]

Daily rallies were held on Cronkeyshaw Common and sizeable public donations to under funds were used to purchase food and clothing. The object was, once more, the Statement Price and nobody who saw the condition of the weavers gathered on the Common could doubt the very real nature of their distress. ''Who'', one speaker at the daily meeting asked, ''could provide a sufficient amount of the coarsest food for their wives and families with such a price for their labour?''[24]

Public sympathy, forfeited to some extent during the periods of disorder, came flooding back. The editor of the *Manchester Times and Gazette* wondered:

> *how these poor weavers and spinners contrive to survive with the trifling pittance the Committee has been able to give them. Still, though suffering in this dreadful manner, they seem determined to have the price they are asking for or perish in the struggle.*[25]

The manufacturers, however, remained unmoved, summoning several weavers before the magistrates ''in order to show cause why they didn't finish or take in their work''.[26]

The weavers replied simply that as the choice appeared to be between prison and starvation, they preferred prison. Public sympathy with the weavers was further increased when James Schofield of Heybrook Mill, who had effectively provoked the crisis, prosecuted a number of his workers, the wife of one of whom ''was at a late stage of pregnancy''.[27]

The Weavers' Association organised a protest march through Rochdale and few uncommitted observers could fail to have been moved by the sight and sound of thousands of weavers and spinners as they thundered down Rochdale's 122 Church Steps in their clogs to a meeting on the Butts.

At this point nearly, but not yet quite, at their lowest ebb, the weavers were given hope from an unexpected source. Robert Owen, the prophet of the Co-operative Movement, is renowned for being the guiding spirit in the attempt to form one national, general trades union. The first attempt at founding a general union, however, was made by Irishman, John Doherty.

Doherty's National Association for the Protection of Labour had been approached by the recently formed Rochdale Trades Committee to address a rally in the town. Doherty's speech on 24 June 1830 was full of beguiling promises, assuring the meeting that, ''support

"Down the Church Steps thundered thousands of striking weavers." The Church Steps as seen around 1860

for the Association would not bring the weavers into conflict with the honourable employers but by uniting together in a general association they would soon strike terror into the hearts of tyrannical and grasping masters."[28] Needless to say, inspired by such rhetoric, the weavers and spinners voted unanimously to join the N.A.P.L.

Subscriptions from the Rochdale weavers poured into the N.A.P.L's coffers at what was, considering their plight, an unbelievable rate: "In the seven weeks between 4 September and 16 October, advertised contributions from Rochdale amounted to a staggering £560 — not far short of half the total volume of subscriptions during that period".[29]

However, on the negotiating front, things were not going well. Faced with the refusal of manufacturers to even begin negotiations at any more than 18s (90p) in the pound on 1824 prices, Doherty was rapidly back-peddaling, recommending now that the weavers "should not attempt a general strike of the whole town but should bring pressure on individual masters in turn."[30] It quickly became apparent to the Rochdale union that the N.A.P.L. had promised far more than it could deliver. More realistic than Doherty they themselves resolved "to abandon for the present all thoughts of a turnout whether partial or general".[31]

In February 1831 a further blow to local confidence in Doherty's enterprise was struck, when it was revealed, in a blaze of publicity, that the Rochdale subscriptions to the N.A.P.L. had been systematically embezzled by one of that organisation's committee members, John Hynes.

The final act of this tragedy was a repeat of the first. The weavers, suffering from yet another round of wage reductions, were again persuaded to approach Doherty who airily recommended that they institute a series of rolling strikes promising, that if the Rochdale weavers required aid, he was sure that "the ready co-operation of the whole union will be well afforded".[32]

Having once more filled the Rochdale union with false hopes, Doherty, "eventually had to realise that their situation was so hopeless that nothing could be achieved by strike action". In its place Doherty recommended a petition to Parliament — a piece of advice, which to a group of individuals who had been involved in every conceivable form of industrial activity over a period of seven years, was both fatuous and insulting.

Disenchanted and embittered, the weavers abandoned all talk of strike action and "finally and completely withdrew from the Association".[33]

There were further flurries of industrial activity in 1833, 1834 and 1837, during a period also remarkable for increased political agitation. Weavers were active in the protests over the new Poor Laws and in the Chartist Movement. Many became followers of Robert Owen and his early vision of Co-operation; many indeed were involved in all these movements and, as we shall see, a weavers' strike in 1844 contributed some of the momentum to the formation of the Rochdale Equitable Pioneers' Society. Finally, it is again worth stressing that, despite all the disappointments and setbacks, self-organisation was becoming a way of working class life.

5. The Charter, The Whole Charter and Nothing But The Charter

As we have seen, during the unrest leading to the passage of the 1832 Parliamentary Reform Act (which effectively gave the vote to the wealthy middle class), local millowners and manufacturers elicited the support of thousands of working class people in Rochdale. The working class, already disillusioned by the limited numbers of people who obtained voting rights in 1832 (687 out of a population of 28,000), were to experience further disappointment in the Parliamentary elections — the first ever for Rochdale as a single constituency — which took place later in the year. At those elections three candidates were put forward.

James Taylor, Unitarian minister and ultra-Radical candidate in the 1832 parliamentary election

The reforming Liberal millowners and manufacturers of the town had selected from their ranks John Fenton, a member of one of the wealthiest local families, which had progressed from woollen manufacturing to merchanting and finally to banking.

The Tories, meanwhile, had approached John Entwisle, a member of the intermarried Entwisle/Royds/Ramsey millowning family group, to represent their interests.

The third candidate was James Taylor, a hat manufacturer from Spotland Bridge, and a preacher of radical politics from the pulpit of the Clover Street Unitarian Chapel (later to become known as the Co-operators' Chapel).

All three candidates presented themselves to a crowd of over 8,000 people on the hustings (a covered cart) outside the Wellington Hotel. Whilst Fenton reflected the moderate reforming aspirations of his colleagues by pledging himself to the "abolition of monopolies, a change in the present Corn Laws, the spread of religious and Civil Liberties and the abolition of the slave trade",[1] Entwisle perplexed the crowd somewhat by merely listing the large number of people who had asked him to stand.

Taylor captured the public mood by announcing a full-blooded radical programme which included, "a total repeal of the Corn Laws, a reduction in taxation, a reduction in the army and navy, a total abolition of the slave trade, annual parliaments, universal suffrage and vote by ballot."[2] The last three, it will be remembered, were on the political agenda from before the days of Peterloo.

When the returning officer, as was the custom of the period, asked the crowd which of the three candidates should become Rochdale's first M.P.:

> *A few hundred hands were held up for Mr. Entwisle and Mr. Fenton, but for Mr. Taylor an immense number were displayed.*[3]

This, however, was merely a cosmetic exercise and Fenton and Entwisle then both demanded, as was their right, a vote by ballot. Considering how few of Taylor's natural constituency were entitled to vote under the 1832 Act, he polled extremely respectably, gaining nearly ⅓ of the votes cast in his home township of Spotland. The final result was, however:

Fenton: 277
Entwisle: 246
Taylor: 109

ROCHDALE
ELECTION.

Wednesday Evening,
12th December, 1832.

STATE OF THE POLL.

Mr. Fenton 238
Mr. Entwisle . . . 220
Mr. Taylor 107

J. WOODS,
POLL CLERK.

State of the 1832 poll on the evening prior to close

The reversal of the popular decision at the hustings reinforced the widespread sense of bitterness and betrayal and Taylor issued an outspoken broadsheet which underlined the breach between his working class supporters and the middle class reformers:

> *It cannot be denied by the public spirit of the show of hands that ... Mr. Taylor was declared the representative of the whole of the public of Rochdale. What strange fatuity it is that the men professing attachment to liberty and sufficiently activated heretofore by the wave of popular applause, should attempt to make themselves a triumph by returning a member in opposition to the wishes of a large majority of their townsmen. But they have triumphed to their own shame and destruction; they have extinguished their influence amongst the working classes for ever ... (because) those who raise all the food, build all the houses, make all the clothes, work all the mines and fight all the battles; those out of whose industry the taxes are paid and the luxuries of the useless few are maintained shall have neither voice nor representation.*[4]

What had also been brought home to ordinary people by the events of 1832 was the power that the vote bestowed — the middle class now had access to the law-making process in Parliament and via such pieces of blatant class legislation as the 1834 Poor Law Amendment Act, they were soon to demonstrate their willingness to manipulate the system for their own benefit.

Consequently, throughout the country, thousands began once more to put their energies towards obtaining a further and far more radical reform of Parliament.

Political activity increased generally but nowhere more so than in the industrial North.

In 1835 Irishman and ultra-radical Feargus O'Connor visited Rochdale and within days of his appearance a Radical Association had been founded. James Taylor was elected president, and Thomas Livsey was appointed the Association's treasurer. Another leading figure was James Leach and as all three were influential figures in the development of local radicalism, it is worth looking briefly at each in turn.

James Leach, born in the weaving community of Spotland Bridge in 1798, was described by Sam Bamford as being of "poor but respectable origins".[5] Like many others from the Spotland Bridge area, Leach became involved in radical politics from an early age and was arrested with Bamford during the Parliamentary Reform protests of 1817. Following his release from prison, Leach incurred Bamford's wrath by accusing him (Bamford) of being a collaborator. To add insult to Bamford's injury, whilst the hero of Peterloo struggled financially, Leach, "with the aid of political friends ... entered into the provision line", becoming one of the leading suppliers of candle tallow and accumulating considerable wealth.[6] There is a strong possibility that amongst Leach's "political friends" were those most radical of middle class manufacturers Thomas and William Chadwick.

Despite his good fortune, Leach did not abandon his political radicalism. In 1840, by this time a committed Chartist, he became the Chief Constable (mayor) of the town and Rochdale became renowned as the venue for major political rallies and demonstrations. As a retailer, however, it must be said that Leach, unlike Thomas Livsey, had little sympathy with the Rochdale Pioneers and was not likely to have been one of the Chartist leaders who paved the way for the establishment of the Co-operative store on Toad Lane.

James Taylor was born at Oakenrod, then just outside the town of Rochdale, in 1787. In the early 1800's he too moved to Spotland Bridge where he established a hatting factory. As one of the radical preachers at the Clover Street Unitarian Chapel, Taylor was very much one of the community he served. His hard-hitting sermons would have had a profound effect on his congregation, a number of whom would later be amongst the 28 (or so) original Rochdale Pioneers.

As we have seen, Taylor stood as the Ultra-radical candidate in the election of 1832 and was later to become the local Chartist leader with the highest national profile. He represented the town at the Chartist's alternative Parliament (the National Convention) and appeared at rallies throughout Lancashire and Yorkshire. After 1848, however, Taylor became disillusioned with local politics, moving to the Unitarian Chapel in nearby Todmorden where he died in 1854.

Thomas Livsey

Thomas Livsey, whose contribution to the development of nineteenth century Rochdale cannot be overstated, was possibly the most extraordinary character the town has produced. Born in 1815, the son of a successful local blacksmith, Livsey was educated in Rochdale until the age of 15 when he was sent to a modest boarding school in Whitchurch. Following his return to Rochdale, he received instructions in flannel weaving from his uncle Robert Schofield, a contemporary of James Taylor and a fellow radical. It was Schofield, who as the organiser of a regular political discussion group, was to be the decisive influence on the young Livsey.

Livsey was not inclined to waste time on business, becoming a less than successful blacksmith and cotton spinner before ending up as an agent for one of the new railway companies. Instead, he devoted his prodigious energies to addressing the problems of the day, acting as a bridge between the middle and working class — whilst always championing the interest of the latter.

Livsey, in his capacity as one of the local Chartist leaders, led the campaign for the extension of voting rights, controlled the direction of the local council and was responsible for the Gas and Water Companies coming under public ownership; he led the local campaign for shorter working hours in the mills and the restriction of child labour and co-ordinated the protests against the new Poor Laws. All in all, he dominated the local political scene for twenty years, influencing the selection of M.P.'s and securing the vote at local level for an unprecedented number of adult males under the Rochdale Improvement Act of 1853.

He was "an out and out man of the people",[7] unpopular with many of the middle class manufacturers (John Bright with whom Livsey frequently crossed swords grudgingly described him on his death as "a diamond, if not highly polished"),[8] but wildly popular with the working class. Finally, he was intimately involved in the initial debate leading to the birth of the local Co-operative Movement and, indeed, became an Arbitrator for the Pioneers in the 1850's. When Livsey died at the early age of 48, the town of Rochdale mourned like it never had before and never would again. At his own request, Livsey was buried next to James Taylor in Rochdale Cemetery.

Taylor, Leach and Livsey, as we have seen, all became dedicated Chartists. Chartism, which grew out of the sort of working class discontent which we have witnessed building up in Rochdale, was a truly national movement based on the belief that working people would be able to improve their standard of life *only* by acquiring the vote. In other words, in order to prosper they must acquire a stake in the system and all other issues and campaigns were merely diversions from the real task.

The aims of the Chartists were encapsulated in their six point charter (hence the name). These six points or demands were:

1. *Universal (male) suffrage — the vote*
2. *Annual Parliaments*
3. *Vote by (secret) ballot*
4. *Abolition of property qualification for M.P.'s*
5. *Payment of M.P.'s*
6. *Equal Electoral Districts.*

With all but the second point achieved (if gradually) over the following eighty years, these demands do not seem particularly outrageous. At the time, however, they were revolutionary and indeed many Chartists were perfectly prepared to achieve their goals through force if constitutional means failed.

The anger and energy which fuelled the Chartist movement were magnified by other issues that further alienated the working classes from their middle class employers. The failure of government to reduce the number of hours worked (particularly by children) in the factories was due, at least in part, to the resistance of millowners such as John Bright; and there was equal popular outrage at the attempt to introduce the new Poor Law into the area.

Briefly, in Rochdale, in common with many other areas in the North-West, the able-bodied poor had traditionally been given cash handouts to tide them over the worst periods of distress. Under the Act of 1834, this was to cease. Instead, the unemployed would be taken to huge "Union" workhouses where families would be broken up and monotonous, grinding and ultimately useless work would be provided for anyone unfortunate enough to end up destitute.

At a torchlight rally in Rochdale on 7 November 1838, national anti-Poor Law campaigner Joseph Raynor Stephens urged his audience to arm themselves in order to resist the implementation of the new Poor Law.

Feargus O'Connor, Chartist leader and founder of the Chartist newspaper the Northern Star

Campaigners such as Stephens, Feargus O'Connor, Thomas Livsey and Todmorden's John Fielden moved easily from one issue to another. On one platform they would call for shorter working hours, on another for the repeal of the Poor Law Amendment Act. Fielden, O'Connor and Livsey, however, increasingly concentrated their energies on campaigning for the vote.

At the same meeting on 7 November, Feargus O'Connor gave his one and only hint as to when a general uprising throughout the country might take place and Stephens' call on local people to arm themselves seems to have been taken seriously. Tory magistrate Clement Royds reported to the Home Secretary that, at the rally:

> *The general topic was subversion to our laws, calling the people to arms and destruction to our magistrates ... I beg to further inform your lordship that regular meetings are held for the purpose of debate, to organise plans to arm the people — that arms are made to a great extent and sold throughout this country — that a cart was brought into this market last Monday laden with firearms and that they were readily sold at very reduced prices — clubs and societies are formed for the purpose of arms — that this population will soon be armed to a very great extent.*[9]

The great debate over the last 150 years has been to what extent these fears were justified. Was Britain on the point of an armed insurrection? For a short time, it seemed as though ordinary people were desperate enough to attempt some form of direct action and certainly, in Rochdale at least, the middle classes had lost control, exerting very little influence over events.

To give one example, in the late 1830's aspiring middle class politicians like John Bright attempted to turn people's attention from the vote to the high price of bread. Manufacturers stood to gain enormously from Free Trade and the removal of tariff barriers on agricultural products such as corn. As these duties in effect contributed to the high price of bread there was, in the second decade of the century, broad agreement between the middle and working classes that the Corn Laws should be abolished.

As Chartist aims became exclusively concentrated on the Six Points, however, Corn Law Repeal became an increasingly middle class preoccupation.

On 2 February 1839, Bright called a public meeting to discuss the Corn Laws and proposed that local manufacturer George Ashworth should chair the debate. James Taylor's counter-proposal that Heywood's "mob-orator" Job Plant should be in the chair "was carried by a large majority". Bright's motion that "it was in the interest of the working classes to assist in calling for a repeal of the Corn Laws"[10] was totally undermined by James Taylor's amendment to the effect that:

> *It is of the opinion of this meeting that though the Corn Laws is an injurious tax, yet the present House of Commons, or any other House of Commons constituted on the present*

suffrage will never repeal the Law and this meeting is of the opinion that the present Corn Law agitation is made up for the purpose of diverting the people from the only remedy for all political grievance: therefore it is necessary that the people must first be in possession of their political rights to affect the repealing of the Corn Laws.[11]

Much to the disgust of the organisers of the meeting, the amendment was carried by an overwhelming majority.

At that meeting, women were once more seen to be playing a leading role and as the Chartist movement adopted a more confrontational stance, women often acted as "shock troops" in the campaigns of civil disobedience, leading processions and demonstrations and, via the Female Radical Association (founded in 1839), providing a forum for working class women to debate the issues of the day in a non-threatening environment.

Anti-Corn Law League Membership Card

Even the normally mildly spoken James Taylor began adopting the language of open conflict. At a major rally on Kersal Moor, to which he had led the Rochdale contingent, Taylor declared that:

> *one of the principles of which the House of Brunswick sat on the throne was the right to resist oppression, and if the House of Brunswick would not admit that principle, it had no right to the throne.*[12]

The veiled threat to overthrow the monarchy was mild in comparison to some of the utterances being made by Chartist leaders. By the summer of 1839 the Chartist National Convention was attempting to organise what is called a Sacred Month —a period of sustained strike activity and mass protest. In preparation for this event, one of the less discreet of the visiting Chartist spokesmen, John Deegan, advised his audience:

> *Arm yourselves with guns and pikes and pistols and get plenty of powder and balls and then you will be ready for the 300 special constables which has (sic) been sworn in by Chadwick and the batch (the magistrates).*[13]

Following this outburst Deegan was promptly, and not altogether surprisingly, arrested by a high percentage of the 300 specials.

In the event, the indecisiveness of the National Convention,the confused and confusing messages being received from the national leadership and the failure to produce an overall strategy, resulted in the collapse of the proposed activities of the Summer of 1839. Only in Newport, in South Wales, in the November of that year, did an abortive attempt at an armed insurrection provide a tantalising glimpse at what may have been planned nationwide.

Although local Chartism undoubtedly received a blow from the failures and disappointments of 1839, the movement was far from finished. Chartists mingled with hungry weavers and followers of Robert Owen at the Weavers' Arms and Socialists' Institute on Yorkshire Street, endlessly debating the issues and searching for practical solutions to their problems. Often, of course, "Owenites", the Chartists, the weavers and the radical nonconformists were one and the same people.

Whilst the Chartists regrouped, the economy took another turn for the worse. Already by 1831, woollen weavers' wages stood at little more than 60% of the level of three years earlier and their income continued to plummet throughout the 1830's.[14] The winter of 1841 was one of terrible severity, prompting local M.P. William Sharman Crawford to draw the attention of the House of Commons to those of his constituents attempting to live on ⅓ of the average wage for working people and possessing "no blanket at all"[15] to cover them at night.

Even Poor Law Commissioner Alfred Tufnell, who had been sent from London to investigate Crawford's claims, could only confirm the level of distress revealing that the appalling conditions affected children, young and middle aged adults and the elderly alike. Yet another report, this one compiled on behalf of the Anti-Corn Law League, provided a number of eyewitness accounts:

> *The house of the woollen weaver was almost proverbial for a degree of comfort and plenty such as is now rarely witnessed. The furniture was abundant, always sufficient and not rarely handsome ... Now we see about us abject poverty on every side. Wages so low that many men with full work are compelled to apply to the Parish for relief; their houses are unfurnished, possessing neither wardrobes nor garments and their hunger-marked countenances bespeak the terrible wrongs they endure.*[16]

Inevitably, as was revealed by local medical practitioners, the people's health was deteriorating rapidly:

> *We the undersigned are of the opinion that, owing to the want of employment and the high price of food, the labouring classes in the Borough of Rochdale … are now suffering great and increasing privations. That they are unable in great numbers to obtain wholesome food in sufficient quantities to keep them in health; and that they are predisposed to disease and rendered unable to resist its attacks … In this respect the population amongst whom we practise are in a much worse state now than they were five or six years ago and for three years past their condition has been gradually sinking and we never knew them in as bad a state at any former period.*[17]

At this juncture, the distress of the weavers (and indeed other sections of the local community) coincided once again with a highly charged political atmosphere. Ominously, as markets further decreased in 1842 and flannels fetched "ruinously low prices",[18] manufacturers began reducing wages.

When, in August 1842, the inevitable strikes began, spreading like wildfire throughout Lancashire, John Bright appeared, at least, to have been taken completely unawares, writing to his brother-in-law:

> *About 2,000 women paraded the town this morning singing hymns. The men are gone to other towns and villages to turn all the hands out. Has the revolution commenced? It looks very probable. The authorities are powerless.*[19]

The methods employed by the strikers were simple but effective. Marching from town to town, they encouraged workers to leave the factories then they pulled the plugs from the steam boilers, halting the machinery and incapacitating the factory.

On 11 August, magistrate William Chadwick, unwilling to use the militia, indulged in the somewhat pointless exercise of swearing in several pensioners as Special Constables in preparation for the arrival of the Royton strikers, by now nicknamed "Plug Dragoons". Consequently, when the Royton contingent arrived, they encountered virtually no opposition. As Bright noted, at the head of the procession (swollen by thousands of local turnouts) which streamed down Drake Street were "women, eight or ten abreast singing lively songs".[20]

Liberal magistrate George Ashworth who had declared himself "prepared to check any excess or breach of the peace", was promptly swept away by a crowd of around 15,000 protestors.[21]

In fact the Liberal magistrates, Ashworth,John Fenton, Henry Kelsall and particularly William Chadwick, were cheered by the crowd. As we have seen, the Chadwicks were deeply affected by events at Peterloo twenty-odd years previously and now the Liberal majority on the magisterial bench, influenced by the Chadwicks, declined the offer of the use of troops.

Meanwhile, shopkeepers in the town, equally sympathetic, threw loaves to the protestors and following the stoppage of Bright's Cronkeyshaw Mill, Jacob Bright senior (John Bright's father and consistently more enlightened an employer than at least two of his sons), "sent for three skips of bread and distributed it amongst the people".[22]

By the end of the day, the strike was complete: "masons, bricklayers, joiners, mechanics and others" had downed tools and an eerie, expectant silence descended on the town.[23] On the following morning representatives from Rochdale were despatched to Whitworth, Colne, Padiham and Heywood whilst another 6,000 strikers marched noisily through Littleborough to Todmorden.

Significantly, what had begun as a strike for the restoration of wage levels soon became a full-blooded call for the Six Points of the Charter. Mass demonstrations were taking place on Cronkeyshaw Common, on Blackstone Edge, on Tandle Hill and on the Butts in the very centre of the town and the cry now was for "The Charter, the whole Charter and nothing but the Charter".[24]

John Bright, on behalf of the manufacturers, called for the strikers to return to work in a particularly patronising speech which ended:

> *An advance of wages to the rate paid in 1840 and ten hours labour per day were the demands you were urged to make. But when the turnout in this district was completed and you had become excited, those demands were abandoned and you were urged to refuse to work until the Charter became law.*[25]

The young John Bright

Or as an anonymous balladeer put it:

> *Then spoke a youth of talents Bright*
> *a champion of the People's right,*
> *"If all the masters in this town*
> *should on their bended knees fall down*
> *and swear that wages should higher run*
> *I say just now it can't be done,"*
> *Then spoke the Chartists, not a few*
> *A labouring man can't get his due*
> *Until the Charter it be got,*
> *This England's not a happy spot.*[26]

An attempt by the millowners to reopen all the factories simultaneously was thwarted by the return of a contingent of Oldham strikers on August 18. Tory magistrate Clement Royds, together with William Chadwick rode with a detachment of 11th Hussars to confront the Oldham marchers at Buersil Bridge. There, the Riot Act was read but "a volley of stones was thrown at the police and Mr. Chadwick was struck on the head with a stone which cut his hat through and almost laid his skull bare".[27]

Thomas Livsey, who was with the crowd, forced himself between the strikers and the unhorsed magistrate. To put it crudely, the volley of missiles had struck the wrong man. Again, to quote a contemporary writer:

> *His good advice was all in vain,*
> *the stones came down like falling rain*
> *His friends around him now are sighing*
> *Oh! William bleeds, oh, he is dying!*
> *His blood around is seen to flow,*
> *A friend is wounded, not a foe.*[28]

And throughout all this, the troops were still not called to intervene! By the following day, the military commanders were so confused at the unexpected and unpredictable behaviour of the Liberal magistrates that they allowed one of that number, Henry Kelsall, to ride unescorted into another company of Oldham strikers and then, assuming that the magistrate had abandoned them, wheeled around and permitted the strikers to pass on. One of the military commanders was of the opinion that the troops, "might as well have been left at the billet"[29] and when the Vicar of Rochdale was curtly informed by William Chadwick that he (the vicar) would not be afforded military protection, the Chancellor of the Duchy of Lancaster was "made aware of the magistrates' extraordinary behaviour".[30]

In due course, the Liberal magistrates were summoned before Lord Derby in order to explain their unmagisterial conduct. Chadwick's split head, acquired in the line of duty, stood him in good stead whilst a strenuous defence from ex-M.P. John Fenton appears to have been sufficient to exonerate himself and his remaining colleagues.

As we have seen, the Chadwicks' fear of a repeat of Peterloo influenced their behaviour, but there were other factors at work which contributed to the magistrates' inaction. Firstly, all four Liberal magistrates were genuinely suspicious of what they regarded as Tory militarism; secondly, all four were inexperienced in crowd control and thirdly, and importantly, the magistrates, like many of their colleagues responsible for local affairs, had been propelled into an uncharacteristically radical position by the increasing status of local Chartists, particularly Thomas Livsey, and the persuasive argument of mass protest.

In this instance, however, the crowd's influence over events was short-lived. As with the extended weavers' strikes of 1830, hunger eventually forced the strikers back to work. In any case, once again, national Chartist leaders were unable to take advantage of the situation, giving neither wholehearted support, nor any sense of direction to the strikers.

Once more, although the Chartist movement did not disappear in 1842, the disappointing outcome of the events of that year, was clearly a major setback. Nevertheless, Thomas Livsey continued to organise and address huge rallies throughout the 1840's and, in 1848, local women made a valiant effort to rekindle the movement. In 1853 Livsey and his colleagues succeeded in establishing a constitution for municipal elections which were virtually the Charter at local level and in 1856 he and other council leaders were branded, "a ragbag of defunct Chartists".[31]

What did die a little in 1842, however, was the notion that the Charter provided the *only* solution for working class ills. Gradually, other avenues were explored as debates among working people broadened out to include such concepts as self-education, self-improvement and Co-operation.

6. "Athenian Democracy"

Before looking at Rochdale as the home of modern Co-operation, it is worth considering two further areas where, at least for a limited period, the crowd had a significant influence over events. Surprisingly, in view of what we have seen so far, non-electors — people without the vote — were able to exert pressure in both municipal and Parliamentary elections, allowing radicals and Chartists to infiltrate into the local power structure.

In the eighteenth century, a number of factors had combined to give the town a unique administrative system with an open populist style and highly-charged political atmosphere. Prior to 1825, as we have seen, local government was concentrated upon the five Townships which comprised the Parish of Rochdale. However, even in the eighteenth century, despite the fact that the power of decision making rested entirely with the local Tory gentry, there was at least *some* public input into the decision making process.

All decisions made behind closed doors had to be taken for ratification to Township meetings and it was the number and nature of those eligible to attend which determined how populist these quarterly sessions were. For instance, in the Township of Hundersfield, the meetings were open to "all leypayers" — in other words, anyone who made a contribution towards the rates, no matter how small. In Spotland Township the invitation was to "all the inhabitants"[1] and generally Township Meetings throughout the Parish involved those on the lower rungs of the social ladder. The ruling élite used this device in order to demonstrate the unanimity of public feeling and therefore persuade other agencies (central government, the Duchy of Lancaster etc.) to recognise and respond to local needs.

Even in 1823, when petitioning parliament to grant the town of Rochdale some degree of self-government, the local gentry — the Vicar, the Lord of the Manor, the magistrates and the leading local families — felt obliged to call a public meeting in order to explain their actions. As a result, the concept of Town, Township and public meetings was incorporated into the new system and survived until well after mid-century. They were used increasingly by radical leadership of the local authority as a means of legitimising their more controversial activities and there is also considerable evidence that public meetings were called in order to pressurise politicians into adopting a more radical programme — a process which prompted one writer to compare the Rochdale system with Athenian Democracy.[2]

Following the Rochdale Police Act of 1825, the town was to be administered by the forerunners of councillors — the Police Commissioners who were defined as "male owners or occupiers of a messuage, house, warehouse or other building ... of the yearly value of at least £35". The Commissioners had powers to widen the streets, establish "watchboxes and watchhouses, employ night patrols and beadles and one or more standing Chief Constable or Constables". They were also empowered to "enter into a contract with the Gas Company in order to light the streets with gas and oil".[3]

Although the £35 property qualification obviously restricted membership to the wealthier section of the community, the fact that there was no election process allowed the more comfortably off radicals such as James Leach to enter the local corridors of power rapidly and without hindrance. Leach took his seat on the Commission as early as July 1832 and by 1837 Leach, Chartists Samuel Holland and Matthew Greenlees, together with long-serving radicals John Dania and Abraham Lord were exerting considerable influence over events. Also present by this date was James Standring, a leading campaigner for the ten hour working day who later gained prominence as one of the Rochdale Pioneers. Thomas Livsey became a Commissioner for the first time on 4 December 1839.[4]

The minute books of the Commissioners reveal that the Liberal reformers, together with the radicals, usually attended the meetings in larger numbers than the Tories by a ratio of around 2:1. By 1835, the volatile nature of the local working class forced the Liberals even more into the radical camp and the first Liberal magistrates in the town were, as we have seen, working almost entirely independently of their Tory counterparts.

In the October of that year the Liberals (John Fenton, George Ashworth and Henry Kelsall) appointed their own magistrates' clerk, William Heaton. When the Tory magistrates refused Heaton permission to consult the law books, "Fenton,Ashworth and Kelsall had no alternative but that of moving to a place where their clerk could perform his duties without annoyance".[5]

In fact, the Liberals went so far as to establish their own office making Rochdale unique in supporting two rival magisterial benches — a formula for complete inertia and total confusion. The situation finally attained the dizzy heights of farce when each set of magistrates began to poach, or virtually kidnap, each others' witnesses. Needless to say, anybody brought before either bench with sympathetic political leanings stood an excellent chance of being dismissed.

Affairs were equally chaotic in the council chamber. In 1840, when the Liberals were unable to decide which of their number should receive the annual honour of becoming the town's Chief Constable (mayor), the Tories, numerically too weak to carry their own candidates, proposed, out of a nice sense of mischief, long-time radical James Leach. Therefore, at the height of Chartist activity in the town, the Tories and Liberals conspired between them to elect a Chartist mayor! No wonder local people believed that their objectives were within reach.[6]

The next stage in the process of creating local anarchy came when 35 Tory Commissioners successfully petitioned the Government for the abolition of Rochdale's independent police force and the introduction of the more efficient but widely detested County Police. The local press was uniformly hostile, the *Manchester Guardian* commenting scathingly:

> *Having publically announced that they would get all local government into their hands and failing in their object, they incur an additional expense at a time when the poor ratepayers are not half fed and many are absolutely starving.*[7]

Simultaneously, Thomas Livsey was waging a vigorous campaign against the Tory controlled Gas Company. When the Directors refused point-blank to negotiate over both supply and pricing policies, Livsey called their bluff and forced a resolution through the Council chamber to the effect that: "As the people are starving and crying out for bread not gas, the streets should no longer be lit at night". It was, therefore, into a town plunged into wintry darkness that the County Police were introduced in November 1841. Not that their task would have been much easier had they entered the town in flaming June — all co-operation was denied them.

Once again, constantly reminded of the strength of public opinion, the Liberal magistrates distanced themselves totally from the County Police and on more than one occasion William Chadwick stormed out of the courtroom when confronted with evidence of the invasions of privacy perpetrated by the Lancashire force. Consequently, as we have seen, the County Police were never called into action during the disturbances of 1842.

Eventually, Rochdale was once more granted powers to establish its own police force and, due largely to the efforts of Thomas Livsey, the Gas Company was brought under municipal control, its pricing policy stabilised and the gas supply extended to virtually every street in the Borough.

During each stage of his campaign against the Gas Company, Thomas Livsey was careful to gauge his level of support by calling public meetings — a device he was to use equally effectively in ensuring, at least for a limited period, that Rochdale's Member of Parliament was as radical as the bulk of his constituents.

Rochdale's first M.P., the Whig/Liberal John Fenton, who, in the popular view had snatched victory in the 1832 election from ultra-radical James Taylor, proved to be totally inept in his first term of office. Had he deliberately set out to antagonise his constituents, he could scarcely have done so more effectively. In voting for the Poor Law Amendment Act, which introduced the Victorian Workhouse system, Fenton succeeded in offending everyone. Even middle class reformers were horrified. Thomas Chadwick expressed the general dismay when he wrote to Todmorden's John Fielden in February 1833: "I feel perfectly ashamed that I have been instrumental in sending a man to Parliament (who)

Rochdale's first M.P., John Fenton, widely denounced for supporting the Poor Law Amendment Act of 1834

ANSWER

To a Friend of the Working Man, and a Non-Elector.

Who Chopped down the People, with a Butcher's Cleaver, for attempting to gain their just Rights?

The Whigs!

Who were the cause of your Fellow Towsmen being slaughtered on the Fifth of May?

The Whigs!!

Who transported your Fellow Workmen for attempting to resist OPPRESSION.

The Whigs!!

Non-Electors,

MAY HEAVEN FORGIVE SUCH MEN!!!

HOLDEN, PRINTER, ROCHDALE.

Tory political handbill from the 1835 election highlighting the short-lived Radical/Tory alliance

voted against honesty and common sense'' and again ''I am afraid our member, Mr. F., will not prove as useful in the House of Commons that I expected he would be''.[8]

The radicals, still led by James Taylor, were blazing mad and whereas, in the next general election, in 1835, most of the reformers rallied immediately to Fenton, the radicals initially threw their support behind John Entwisle, the Tory candidate. Taylor, thoroughly disillusioned by the events of 1832, did not stand but pledged himself to the Tory nominee rather than be associated with Fenton.

When, therefore, ''the Liberals called a meeting to consider how far the working classes were interested in reform ... a large number of Mr. Entwisle's supporters marched behind the banner of the ultra-radical party''.[9] Infuriated by this turn of events, the Liberals attacked the Tory parade, seized the radical banner and tore it to shreds. ''Mr. Entwisle's party retaliated with a shower of stones and a desperate fight ensued''.[10]

On the day of the nominations, scores of his supporters from 1832 marched behind Taylor from Spotland Bridge to the town centre. At the last moment (or maybe it had all been a calculated ploy to warn the reformers of public discontent with their candidate), Taylor joined Fenton's procession as it made its way to the Wellington Hotel.

Moreover, Taylor was persuaded to propose Fenton before the crowd at the hustings, thus legitimising the reform candidate, in principle at least, as the people's choice. As a result of this, Entwisle, who in 1832 had confined his electoral address to a list of those people who had nominated him, now concentrated "almost exclusively to a censure of Mr. James Taylor for having joined the opposite party".[11]

Not all radicals, however, could be persuaded to forgive Fenton, and Entwisle, by virtue of a split in his opponent's ranks, was returned by 369 votes to 326.The overall lesson of the 1835 election from the Liberal/reformers perspective was obvious: they desperately needed the wholehearted support of the radical electors and that of the increasingly disenchanted "Non-Electors".

In effect, the Non-Electors were the town meeting, the general public, in political guise. Denied the vote by the constitution of 1832, this numerically strong, but politically impotent body manipulated the imperfect electoral system to their own advantage. As the vote was not secret, it was a matter of public record who voted for whom and from 1837 (at least) onwards the "Non-Electors" published this information for general consumption. Therefore, although employers could

The Whig reformers view of Tory "excesses"

influence their employees to vote in certain ways, the "crowd" had a similar (if not as potent) hold over local tradesmen. This weapon in their armoury was known as "Exclusive Dealing" or, in other words, "If you don't vote for my candidate, I won't use your grocers', butchers', tea shop etc."

As most Non-Electors were, during this period at least, radical sympathisers "Exclusive Dealing" tended to benefit the radicals or the Chartists as opposed to the less adventurous Liberal reformers, otherwise known — disparagingly by this time — as "the Whigs". The difference between the two camps was defined by the then ultra-radical *Rochdale Observer*:

> *Ever since the first blunder which the Whig electors made in returning a Tory member for this Borough, there have existed two parties in the town antagonistic to each other with regard to general and local policy ... The Whig reformers, unable to go the length of the staunch radical, knew it to be in their interest to meet the democracy of the latter half-way ... Moreover, when the Corn Law agitation was rife, none more so than they preached up an identity of interest or were louder in their protestation of right feelings towards the industrial artisan. "Let us pull together", they said, "for a repeal of the Corn Laws and we will help you get your political existence hereafter" ... While, however, they were lavishing kisses on our cheeks, they were prompted by the feelings of a Judas and the cloven hoof has at length become unmasked.*[12]

Wading through the sea of mixed metaphors, the significance of the above piece lies in the importance attached to the gulf between the reformers and the radicals and the continuing sense of betrayal experienced by the working classes. Indeed, when John Entwisle died in 1837, it was only with the greatest reluctance that the radicals were persuaded that John Fenton, as the sitting member, would be the strongest candidate.

The Tories selected banker and magistrate Clement Royds, who did little to endear himself to the public at the hustings, with the following exchange:

> q: *Are you willing to vote for election by ballot?*
> a: *It is quite out of the question, I hope to never see it.*
> q: *Are you willing to vote for an extension of the suffrage.?*
> a: *No.*[13]

At least the radicals knew where they stood with that and John Fenton went on to win the election with a majority of 44. In 1840, however, Fenton announced his retirement, a decision which caused the radicals to shed few tears. The Liberals, who had for electoral purposes, organised themselves into a Reform Association, decided to nominate a moderate reformer from outside the Borough, Milner Gibson, as their candidate.

The radicals had other ideas. Thomas Livsey promptly organised a meeting of the Non-Electors to oppose the nomination. As we have seen, the economic conditions in the early 1840's were appalling; the political temperature was rising and Livsey was therefore able to call upon ordinary people to challenge the selection.

The nominee of the radicals was the ultra-radical Irishman William Sharman Crawford and this decision was then presented to the Reform Association as a fait accompli. Unsurprisingly, "the more wealthy Liberals did not approve of the selection" but rather than risk another disastrous three-way split and let in the Tories once more, the reformers reluctantly agreed to ratify the radicals' choice.[14]

The Tories had selected as their candidate John Fenton's brother, James (it was not unknown for some of the wealthier families to have divided political loyalties), and the battle lines were drawn.

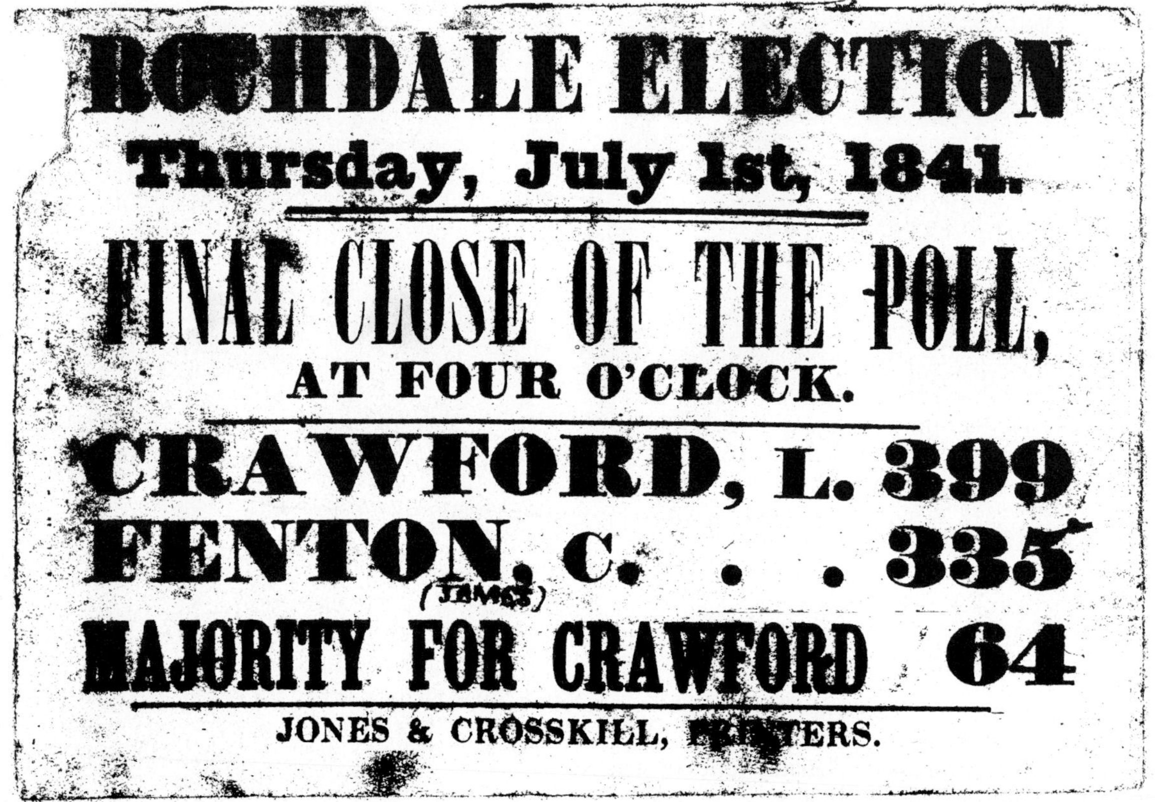

ROCHDALE ELECTION
Thursday, July 1st, 1841.
FINAL CLOSE OF THE POLL,
AT FOUR O'CLOCK.
CRAWFORD, L. 399
FENTON, C. . . . 335
MAJORITY FOR CRAWFORD 64
JONES & CROSSKILL,

Final result of the 1841 poll

Both parties used sections of the working classes as political shock-troops. Crawford's procession to the hustings was led "by a large body of Irishmen",[15] whilst Fenton and his supporters paraded behind "the courageous colliers of Smallbridge",[16] given the day off for the occasion by the Lord of the Manor and widely perceived as being "only partially civilized". Within minutes of the rival groups meeting, "partisans on either side belaboured each other with sticks and other weapons" after which, "a frightful encounter ensued and raged for about ten minutes".[17]

When peace was eventually restored, a poll was demanded by both candidates, Crawford emerging the victor by 399 votes to 335. Throughout the period of Chartist unrest, Crawford remained a favourite with the working class and was returned unopposed as the town's M.P. in 1847.

Although it is easy to exaggerate the degree of power wielded during this period by ordinary people, it is nevertheless true to say that during the 1830's and 1840's, they were able, even if indirectly, to exert, by sheer weight of numbers, considerable influence over events. Conversely, however, circumstances were still very much against them. Poverty and ill-health were the norms for the vast majority of the people of the town and there was a desperate need for some institution or organisation which could provide an alternative vision of society together with the promise of self-improvement whilst, at the same time, addressing some of the practical problems of the day.

7. Owenites and Socialists — Towards A Co-operative Commonwealth

The store opened by the Rochdale Equitable Pioneers Society on Toad Lane in December 1844 was not the first Co-op in Britain — that honour probably goes to the dockers of Chatham and Woolwich who began a society as early as 1760 — nor was it even the first Co-operative store on Toad Lane! In 1833, striking flannel weavers, instead of merely downing tools, went into competition with their employers. In addition to selling finished cloth on the open market, the Rochdale Friendly Co-operative Society opened a small shop, selling provisions to a restricted number of members. The Friendly Co-operative Society had close ties with the Rochdale Journeymen Weavers' Association and, as we have seen, the weavers were involved in a lengthy series of strikes and lockouts throughout the 1830's.

This close link between early Co-operation and trades unionism was a reflection of national events and owed much to the life and work of the remarkable Robert Owen — the inspiration behind the Co-operative movement.

Born in Newtown, Montgomeryshire in 1771, Owen had, by 1799, become a master cotton spinner in Manchester. Having subsequently bought a complex of cotton mills at New Lanark in Scotland, Owen soon learned that his employees responded more positively to sympathetic and humane management than they did to the normal heavy-handed (and sometimes downright cruel) mill discipline. As he improved conditions at New Lanark, opening a school and a shop on the premises, Owen's convictions gradually evolved into a personal philosophy.

Owen's views were based on the premise that it is people's environment which governs their behaviour and that by providing decent housing and free education for all and, most importantly, by ensuring that ordinary people shared in the profits of their labour, competition would be eliminated and a classless, caring society would result.

Robert Owen, the prophet of Co-operation

In 1817 Owen published a number of "plans for the creation of villages of Co-operation" where everyone would live and work in harmony and from which in time a "New Moral World" or "Co-operative Commonwealth" would evolve. There was to be no violent upheaval or revolution leading to the creation of the Commonwealth; instead the concept would spread gradually until capitalism was eliminated. Owen envisaged the individual communities being established by wealthy philanthropists, and indeed several benign capitalists were persuaded to contribute to a number of schemes in the 1820's and 1830's.

Such notions were obviously attractive to ordinary working people. It has already been mentioned that during this period industrial capitalism was an extremely unstable system, subject to wild fluctuations and unpredictable "boom-slump cycles" which threw people out of work in their thousands and reduced whole areas of the country to near-starvation level before lurching back to profitability and near full employment.

During the periods of depression, manufacturers resorted to imposing wage reductions and working people soon realised that they were not benefitting from their investment (i.e. their labour) in the good times and were cast aside when the economy collapsed. "Owenism", Co-operation or Socialism (in other words socially beneficial experiments) appeared to offer a viable alternative and the vision of the New Moral World was certainly more attractive than the reality of the old, decidedly immoral one.

Whilst Robert Owen was in the U.S.A., attempting to establish colonies on the other side of the Atlantic, some of his notions were being challenged and modified by a Dr. William King of Brighton. King, who in 1828 had founded the extremely influential journal *The Co-operator*, was committed to the creation of colonies, but disagreed with Owen as to how they should be founded. Owen had never advocated the establishment of Co-operative stores. His was a far broader vision. Shops and stores, he believed, all too often became an end in themselves. Similarly, he had always maintained that the Villages of Co-operation should be directly funded by wealthy philanthropists.

King's proposals were based firmly on the concept of working class self-help and the Co-operative store was an integral part of his plan. Workers would be encouraged to donate a small amount on a regular basis until enough capital had been raised to start a shop. A limited range of goods would then be sold to members, until there was a sufficient surplus to subsidise the production (by the unemployed) of consumer goods for resale. As profits accrued, factories would be established, land would be purchased ad via this evolutionary process, the Co-operative Commonwealth would be achieved.

Between 1826 and 1835 more than 250 Co-operative Societies were founded. In 1832 the handloom weavers who began the Rochdale Friendly Co-operative Society circulated a document to others in the woollen trade which highlighted the local circumstances:

> *The Rochdale Friendly Co-operative Society beg leave to solicit the encouragement of their Co-operative brethren in the flannel manufacturers. In consequence of the unprecedented desperation of the flannel trade, several of the members have been thrown out of employment and in order to rescue them from actual starvation, the society has been induced to start manufacture on an extensive scale in the above business in the confident expectation of support of their fellow Co-operators.* [1]

And, as we have seen, in the following year the Friendly Society, which included future Rochdale Pioneers Charles Howarth and James Standring, opened a store

Early buildings in Toad Lane, Rochdale — the town's first Co-operative store was located in similar premises

at 15 Toad Lane. Very much influenced by national developments, inspired and ideologically fuelled by the ideas of Robert Owen and others, the store survived for two years before being forced to close. The collapse, it has been argued, was due to the fact that Society tolerated, or even encouraged, credit trading. However, the confusion caused by Owen's increasingly controversial and eccentric beliefs, also contributed — as did the movement's close links with trades unionism.

Although it is possible to over emphasise Robert Owen's direct influence on trade associations (as we have seen, the majority of strikes in Rochdale revolved around the maintenance of a piece rate or Statement Price), nevertheless a continuing debate took place locally which linked Owen's new view of society with the plight of the handloom weavers.

In the North of England, John Doherty was organising his National Association for the Protection of Labour and this first attempt at a general trades union drew heavily for its support on the Rochdale area. The more directly Owenite-inspired Grand National Consolidated Trades Union engendered little interest in a workforce disillusioned by the collapse of Doherty's venture.

Nationally, however, when the Grand National Consolidated failed, Co-operation suffered a heavy blow, Co-operative stores closing throughout the country. Owen himself drifted away from trades unions towards increasingly vague and visionary notions of his New Moral World. Owenism became a sect with social missionaries sent out to convert working people and Social or Socialists' Institutes were opened throughout the country. With the establishment of the Rational Society, these Owenite Socialists had a national stage on which to debate the broad philosophical issues. Many of them rejected Owen's dressing up of his doctrine as a new religion and were seeking more practical solutions to their problems.

By 1838, many of the factors which led to the modern Co-operative Movement being founded in Rochdale already existed. We have seen how ordinary people had learned self-organisation and leadership from nonconformist chapels and trades unionism and had begun to experiment with Chartism and other alternative social systems. Also in that year, the Socialists' Institute was established.

Significantly, the Institute was an annex to the Weavers' Arms on Yorkshire Street where handloom weavers,Chartists and local radicals already mingled. Amongst these were James Taylor, members of his congregation from the Clover Street Chapel and Thomas Livsey.The interconnection of the various movements is illustrated by the fact that Poor Law agitator, short-time advocate, Church Rate opponent, radical Commissioner and Chartist leader, Thomas Livsey, was also treasurer of the Socialists' Institute.

Based at the Institute, members of the Rochdale branch of the Rational Society (Branch No. 24), were becoming alienated from what they regarded as Robert Owen's personal spiritual quest and were aligning themselves with the more down-to-earth views of one G.J. Holyoake (later the historian of the Rochdale Pioneers). Holyoake firmly believed that any and all Co-operative communities should be established and run by social equals under self-governing conditions — a view firmly endorsed by local veterans of Co-operation such as Charles Howarth and James Standring.

Two further factors inspired Howarth and his companions to devise their new principles of Co-operation. The first of these dated back to the early years of the century — the establishment by unscrupulous manufacturers of the detested Truck Shops. Despite the success enjoyed by the Weavers' Union in forcing the closure of several such institutions in the 1830's, the practise continued, particularly in times of economic decline. Not only were the goods provided for the weavers in lieu of wages expensive in cash terms, they were also of extremely poor quality. Both inside and outside the Truck Shop, it was common to adulterate food with additives. Sugar and salt were mixed with white sand, chalk was added to cheese, anything that could be diluted with water was, and coffee often contained quantities of earth and mud. In addition, meat was usually bad and potatoes and other vegetables quite simply rotten. There were even incidences of beer being "cut" with arsenic!

Another equally unpopular retail outlet was the Badger Shop where the unlimited credit offered to the poverty stricken townsfolk did nobody any favours.

The second factor contributing to the devising of the Rochdale Principles and the opening of the store on

Toad Lane, was the continuing social unrest and the role in that unrest played by the Chartists. G.J. Holyoake in his history of the Rochdale Pioneers gives little credit to the Chartist movement in the development of Co-operation. However, while it is true that for a number of years the view was that Chartism was the *only* solution to the problems of working people, and that any other movements were distractions, nevertheless in the Rochdale of the early 1840's, there was a willingness to broaden out the debate and it is now clear that it was the Chartists who were the prime movers in the early discussions leading to the opening of the store on Toad Lane.

At least eight of the Rochdale Pioneers were active Chartist sympathisers and as Ambrose Tomlinson, Chartist, Co-operator and afterwards a member of the Independent Labour Party recalled:

> *Co-operation originated not from a weavers' strike but from the old Chartist Movement. The Chartists had begun to hold meetings in a room at the corner of Penn Street. At these meetings Co-operation was talked about. The secretary was Mr. Thomas Livsey ... They were discussing Co-operation in 1841 and in 1842 some of the members began to pay 3d per week in order to accumulate funds in connection with a Co-operative scheme ... After a while there was a quarrel, the Co-operators in the Society seceded and some of them were amongst the members of the Pioneers' Co-operative Society.*[2]

In support of this view, the *Manchester Guardian* of 17 December 1842 reported: "The Chartists intended opening a Co-operative store in order to check the shopkeepers who opposed them",[3] and another leading Co-operator of the 1840's, Abraham Greenwood, also

Fourteen of Rochdale's pioneering Co-operators, portrayed in 1865

emphasised the role of the Chartists: "It started with the Chartists ... It really was a social movement with the idea of bettering the conditions of the people".[4]

The final catalyst, however, was the local economic crisis of 1844. As the economy nosedived, the manufacturers resorted to the time-honoured tactic of reducing wages. And as they had done for the last twenty years, weavers demanded a return to the negotiated piece rates. Some manufacturers agreed but only on the condition that the new wage levels were accepted by all of their number and as this was decidedly not the case, there was deadlock once again. The weavers fell back on the gambit of the rolling strike and the woollen industry slowly ground to a halt.

Unemployed weavers gravitated towards the Socialists' Institute and whilst not all of the Pioneers were weavers, at least 19 out of the original 28 (or so) described themselves as such. What emerged from the sessions there and elsewhere was a new synthesis of the principles of Co-operation. The establishment of a new society was still the overall objective, the first stage of which was the opening of a shop. With their combination of Owenite and Chartist tenets, the Rochdale Principles were a unique blend of idealism and common sense.

Although the Principles, still the basis for Co-operative trading worldwide, were not written down at the time, they can be summarised as:

— *Democratic Control, one member one vote and equality of the sexes.*
— *Open Membership.*
— *A fixed rate of interest payable on investment.*
— *Pure unadulterated goods with full weights and measures given.*
— *No credit.*
— *Profits to be divided pro-rata on the amount of purchase made (the dividend).*
— *A fixed percentage of profits to be devoted to educational purposes.*
— *Political and religious neutrality.*

From Chartism, therefore, the Pioneers adopted the principle of one member one vote, whilst Owenism gave the wider vision of the Co-operative Commonwealth and the emphasis on education.

In fact, none of the Rochdale Principles was in themselves new — not even the dividend on purchase or "divi". However, historian G.D.H. Cole was adamant that this took nothing away from Charles Howarth and his fellow Pioneers. As he said, "the novelty lay not in the notion of the dividend by itself, but in bringing it into the right relationship to the other Principles".[5]

After all the perspiration and inspiration which had gone into devising the Principles, the Pioneers had equal difficulty in locating a premises. Eventually a warehouse was found at 31 Toad Lane and approximately half of the money obtained so far from the 28 (or thereabouts) original subscriptions was spent on fitting the shop out with counters, shelves, scales and weights. The rest was used to buy "flour, oatmeal, sugar, butter and candles at wholesale prices which were sold to members at retail rates".

The Socialists' Institute on Yorkshire Street, the meeting place of Chartists and Co-operators

The store opened on 21 December 1844 — legend has it to crowds of hostile rival shopkeepers, grinning youths and anxious members. Abraham Greenwood, however, put these early days into perspective in a subsequent newspaper interview:

> — *Wasn't there a good deal of opposition at the start?*
> — *No, people looked upon us as being far too insignificant.*
> — *But the shopkeepers didn't like it did they?*
> — *The shopkeepers began their opposition too late. We were well established when they started to get their back up about us.*[6]

Greenwood also described the layout of the shop and put the record straight over the comparative importance of the "divi".

> — *You only started with groceries didn't you?*
> — *Practically all groceries. We only used one side of the shop. The back we used as a store room. We had the ground floor. The second floor was a Sunday school and the top storey was Bethel Chapel. The idea of paying dividends to the members scarcely occupied our thoughts at the beginning. We thought we were doing well if we maintained our ground.*[7]

As Greenwood indicated, the Pioneers initially made slow progress. From the traditionally accepted figure of 28 members in 1844, the Society grew to 74 members in 1845 with only a further 6 added to the books in the following year. In 1847 there were 110 registered members, rising to 140 by the end of 1848.

It was with the collapse of the Rochdale Savings Bank in 1849 that the Society took off, achieving a

The Toad Lane Store as it opened in 1844

membership of 390 by the end of the year. The Savings Bank incident is extremely significant. For decades, the town's middle class had been attempting to implant notions of "thrift and good housekeeping upon the working people", even going so far as to sponsor a savings bank for any small amount of excess in the family budget. The bank was supposedly underwritten by a group of major manufacturers and overseen on a day-to-day basis by millowner George Howarth.

Hundreds had invested their meagre capital in the bank when the bombshell dropped that Howarth had been embezzling the funds in order to prop up his ailing business. When the bank's trustees, including reformist millowners George Ashworth and Henry Kelsall, offered only partial compensation they were left in little doubt as to why their offer was unacceptable:

> *1st Because you have allowed your names to be held forth to us as sufficient guarantee of the security of our deposits.*
> *2nd Because your acceptance of the office of Trusteeship implied a*

> *voluntary taking upon yourselves the duty of protecting our savings and failing that duty ... you render yourselves morally if not legally bound ...to make good the deficiency.*
> *3rd Because your wilful neglect as Trustees has caused the deficiency.*
> *4th Because it is unjust to shift your own responsibilities on the shoulders of working men ... and would collaborate the feelings amongst them that your class is ever ready to oppress and despoil the poor.*[8]

The Savings Bank was not re-established, only partial compensation was ever received by the investors and working people searched for some institution over which they could exercise personal control and where their money was in safe hands — their own. They turned to the Rochdale Equitable Pioneers Society.

Another direct result of this latest evidence of middle-class treachery was a deep and lasting suspicion of *all* institutions sponsored by their "betters" for the supposed benefit of ordinary people. Thus, whereas middle class educational establishments (the Literary and Philosophical Society, the Atheneum, the Lyceum) withered and died, the Pioneers Library and Education Department (founded by Abraham Greenwood in 1849) went from strength to strength. As a correspondent to the local press wrote in 1861, "The Mechanics Institutes rely on donations and subscriptions from the rich but no such aid is solicited or has been received by the Pioneers".[9]

Consequently, Rochdale never supported a Mechanics Institute and when middle class self-help advocate Samuel Smiles visited the town, "his listeners were exceedingly scanty, so much so that we believe he will not repeat his visit".[10]

Meanwhile the Rochdale Equitable Pioneers flourished until, by 1860, the membership was nearly 3,500, the financial stability of the Store was guaranteed and the Pioneers were extending into other fields. Shops based on the Rochdale Principles proliferated, firstly in neighbouring towns, then throughout the North and nationwide.

Rochdale became and remains the Mecca for Co-operators from all over the world, but lest it be forgotten, the Rochdale Pioneers left other equally important legacies:

Property Rights for Women

Prior to 1870, a married woman's property — money, land, everything — belonged legally to her husband. The Pioneers with their Principle of Equality of membership made no distinction between the sexes. When the then Home Secretary was investigating this issue he despatched his private secretary, Albert Rutson, to Rochdale. There Rutson discovered that if a man demanded his wife's dividend, share or any other investment in the Pioneers' Society, he was refused and the woman informed. At the time this practise was clearly illegal, but when the Married Woman's Property Act was finally passed in 1870, it was largely due to Rutson's conversion by the Rochdale Equitable Pioneers.

A Lasting Example of Religious Toleration

Many of the original Pioneers were members of the Clover Street Unitarian Chapel, others were Swedenborgians, still others were atheists. These affiliations counted for nothing. The Pioneers insisted upon tolerance in religion as in all else.

The Establishment of a national organisation, to support, encourage and promote Co-operative Principles

This was the Co-operative Union, begun in 1867 by Abraham Greenwood, William Cooper, James Smithies and Charles Howarth from the Pioneers, together with representatives from neighbouring towns.

A blueprint for Co-operative Wholesaling

The original Co-operative wholesaling experiment began in Rochdale in 1855 after other societies had approached the Pioneers for assistance in obtaining supplies.

Educational Opportunities for all

Education was the mainstay of nineteenth century Co-operation. Reading rooms proliferated, libraries were established,lectures and courses were organised, leading directly to the creation of the Adult School and the Workers' Educational Association at the turn of the century.

An Alternative to Competitiveness in the Market place

Co-operation offers an alternative to competitive trading. It had and continues to have, a particular attractiveness for emerging economies.

A Separate Co-operative Guild for Women

In 1883, nearly forty years on from the establishment of the Pioneers, the Co-operative Women's Guild was founded, representing the interests of thousands of female Co-operators throughout the country.

A Collective Approach to Problem Solving

Although some would have us believe that there is no such thing as society, the story of the Rochdale Pioneers tells us different. Drawing on their experience from all the social experiment that had gone before, the Pioneers evolved a system of mutual support which benefitted and still benefits millions of ordinary people worldwide.

Expansion! Building the new Central Store for the Rochdale Equitable Pioneers Society in 1864

So why, after all that has been said, was the modern Co-operative Movement born in Rochdale rather than elsewhere? As we have seen, the answer lies partly in the town's geographical location on the Lancashire/Yorkshire border making it a "clearing house for ideas". Another factor is the town's comparative antiquity. Rochdale was not, like some neighbouring towns, entirely a product of the Industrial Revolution. It therefore had well- established customs and traditions and tended not to be as volatile as some of the surrounding areas. Issues were debated and discussed at great length and the insatiable intellectual curiosity was combined with a practical approach to problem solving.

The survival of wool and flannel as staple industries into the mid-nineteenth century meant that there remained in the area thousands of handloom weavers, reduced in circumstances but increasingly self-educated and desperately seeking solutions to their economic and social problems.

They, together with other workers, immersed themselves in chapels, clubs, societies and organisations and the overwhelmingly working class complexion of the town (combined with the comparatively small size of local mills) made it difficult for the middle class to exert control

Also, although the development of Co-operation should not be viewed as the logical end of an evolutionary process, there is no doubt that the experience gained from their involvement in trades unionism and Chartism and other lessons learned in self-organisation were invaluable in converting Robert Owen's philosophy into a practical reality.

None of the above, taken individually, explains why Rochdale rather than, say, Oldham or Bury gave birth to Modern Co-operation. However, in total they do go some way to providing an answer. Perhaps, at the end of the day, however, it is sufficient to credit the genius of those ordinary local people, the Rochdale Pioneers who were:

Charles Howarth	*Warper*	*Oldham Road*
James Day	*Joiner*	*John Street*
John Bent	*Tailor*	*John Street*
James Tweedale	*Clogger*	*Barnish Lane*
James Smithies	*Woolsorter*	*Drake Street*
Joseph Smith	*Woolsorter*	*Water Street*
William Lee	*Weaver*	*Spotland Bridge*
John Whitehead	*Weaver*	*School Lane*
James Holt	*Weaver*	*Greenwood Street*
Robert Barkley	*occupation not known*	*Flannel Street*
Edward Fitton	*Weaver*	*Victoria Place*
George Ashworth	*Weaver*	*South Lane*
Bengamin Brierley	*Weaver*	*Pinfold*
John Lomax	*Weaver*	*Milkstone*
Joe Crabtree	*Weaver*	*Toad Lane*
William Taylor	*Weaver*	*Shawclough*
Samuel Ashworth	*Weaver*	*High Street*
John Holt	*Weaver*	*Redcross Street*
James Standring	*Weaver*	*Entwisle Place*
James Lord	*Weaver*	*Mount Pleasant*
Miles Ashworth	*Weaver*	*Spotland Bridge*
Abraham Taylor	*Weaver*	*School Lane*
James Maden	*Weaver*	*Moss Lane*
James Knowles	*Weaver*	*Mount Pleasant*
Abraham Holt	*Weaver*	*Oak Street*
James Manock	*Weaver*	*Spotland Bridge*
Samuel Ashworth	*Warehouseman*	*Spotland Bridge*
William William	*Overlooker*	*address not known*
William Cooper	*Weaver*	*Lowerplace*
Benjamin Rudman	*Pedlar*	*Shawclough*
William Mellalieu	*Spinner*	*Jackybrow*[11]

These then, together with fellow local Co-operators, John Collier, David Brooks, John Snowcroft, Charles Barnish, John Garside, George Healey, James Wilkinson and John Lord, the thousands of unnamed men and women who paved the way for them, and not forgetting the ubiquitous Thomas Livsey, changed the course of modern history — for the better. They were all, in their way, Rochdale Pioneers.

Notes

Introduction

1. Hobsbawm, E.J., The Age of Revolution. p.261
2. Cole, G.D.H., A Century of Co-operation. p.40

1 FROM MARKET TO MILL TOWN

1. Bamford, S., Tim Bobbin's Tummus and Mary. 1850 pp.IV-V
2. Population statistics extrapolated from Census information for the Parish of Rochdale.
3. Analysis of 1841 Census of Population.

2 CHURCHES AND CHAPELS

1. Religion Census, 1851 analysed with population statistics.
2. Church and Chapel register, Rochdale Local Studies.
3. Cole, G.D.H., A Century of Co-operation. p.42
4. Ibid. p.55
5. Baines,E., Social Educational and Religious state of the Manufacturing Districts.
6. Manchester Guardian, 29 July 1840
7. Ibid. 8 August 1840
8. Ibid. 23 January 1841
9. Ibid. 22 May 1841
10. Ibid.
11. Rochdale Sunday School Minute Book, 20 October 1806
12. Ibid. 14 December 1814
13. Standring, R., Sunday schools among the Mountains as they were fifty years Ago. 1874 pp.13-14

3 BREAD RIOTS AND SHUTTLE GATHERING

1. Contemporary verse quoted in Rochdale Observer article 16 January 1908
2. The Times, 7 January 1808
3. Contemporary unidentified newspaper cutting, Rochdale Local Studies.
4. Bamford, S., Passages in the Life of a Radical p.35
5. The Courier, 29 July 1819
6. Contemporary unidentified newspaper cutting, Rochdale Local Studies.
7. Ibid.
8. Unpublished letter Thomas Chadwick to Charles Chadwick, Rochdale Local Studies.
9. Robertson, W., Social and Political History of Rochdale p.157

4 MIDNIGHT MISCHIEF

1. Series of letters by John Tester, Leader of the Bradford Woolcombers to the Leeds Mercury, June, July 1824
2. Hammond, J.L. and Hammond, B., The Skilled Labourer p.132 (The preamble to the Weavers' document ended "in order that you may become men and consider your own importance to the trade")
3. Handbill, Rochdale Local Studies.
4. Combination Laws, Select Committee report 1825 p.151
5. Ibid. p.159
6. Home Office Disturbance Papers H.O. 40/19. Document 174
7. Ibid. Document 221
8. Handbill, Rochdale Local Studies.
9. Rochdale Recorder, 3 February 1827
10. Manchester Guardian, 17 January 1827
11. Rochdale Recorder, 19 May 1827
12. Ibid. 15 September 1827
13. Handbill, Rochdale Local Studies.
14. Open letter (broadsheet), Rochdale Local Studies.
15. Rochdale Recorder, 26 January 1828
16. Ibid.
17. Ibid.
18. Handbill, Rochdale Local Studies.
19. Robertson, W., History of Rochdale Past and Present, p.306
20. Manchester Guardian, 5 September 1829
21. Ibid.
22. Robertson, W., History of Rochdale ... op.cit., p.308
23. Manchester Guardian, 11 May 1830
24. Manchester Times and Gazette, 22 May 1829
25. Ibid. 5 June 1830
26. Ibid.
27. Ibid. 19 June 1830
28. United Trades Co-operative Journal. July 1830 p.153
29. Kirby, R.G. and Musson, A.E., Voice of the People p.178
30. Ibid. p.180
31. Manchester Guardian, 30 October 1830
32. Kirby and Musson, op.cit., p.211
33. Ibid.

5 THE CHARTER, THE WHOLE CHARTER AND NOTHING BUT THE CHARTER

1. Robertson, W., Social and Political History, op.cit., p.169
2. Ibid. p.170
3. Ibid. p.186
4. Ibid. p.189
5. Bamford, S., Passages in the Life of a Radical p.160
6. Ibid. p.161
7. Rochdale Observer, 15 October 1864
8. Ibid. (Letter from John Bright), 6 February 1864
9. Home Office Disturbance Papers H.O. 40/37/828
10. Robertson, W., Life and Times of John Bright pp.72-3
11. Ibid.
12. Manchester Guardian, 13 March 1839
13. Home Office Disturbance Papers. H.O. 40/37/828 (Deegan is also reported as saying, "if Universal Suffrage is not given to us by the Government, we will have it by force")
14. From the Report of the Anti-Corn Law Delegates to the Conference in Manchester, 1842. Reprinted in Robertson, W., Life and Times. op.cit.
15. Manchester Guardian, 25 September 1841
16. Robertson, W., Life and Times op.cit., pp.127-130
17. Ibid.
18. Northern Star, 21 May 1842
19. Unpublished Correspondence 12 August 1842. Rochdale Local Studies.
20. Robertson,W., Life and Times. op.cit., pp.136-140
21. Manchester Guardian, 13 August 1842
22. Robertson, W., Life and Times, op.cit.
23. Ibid.
24. Manchester Guardian, 13 August 1842
25. Robertson, W., Life and Times. op.cit., p.140
26. The Turnout for the Battle of Buersil Bridge. Rochdale Local Studies.
27. Rose, A.G., Truckling Magistrates of Lancashire in Transaction of the Lancashire and Cheshire Antiquarian Society. Vol. 83 (1985)
28. The Turnout ... op.cit.
29. Rose. A.G. op.cit.
30. Ibid.
31. Broadsheet, Rochdale Local Studies.

6 ATHENIAN DEMOCRACY

1. Hundersfield and Spotland Township Poor Rate Books,Rochdale Local Studies.
2. Garrard, J., Leadership and Power in Three Victorian Towns. p.117
3. Rochdale Police Act 1825
4. Minute Books, Rochdale Police Commissioners.
5. Manchester Guardian, 5 November 1839
6. Ibid. 8 May 1841
7. Ibid. 24 November 1841
8. Correspondence Thomas Chadwick to John Fielden, February 1833, Rochdale Local Studies.
9. Robertson, W., Social and Political History op.cit., p.207 and following
10. Ibid.
11. Ibid.
12. Rochdale Observer, 10 May 1856
13. Robertson, W., Social and Political History op.cit. p.241
14. Ibid. p.321
15. Ibid. p.335
16. Ibid.
17. Ibid.

7 OWENITES AND SOCIALISTS: TOWARDS A CO-OPERATIVE COMMONWEALTH

1. J.T.W. Mitchell quoting the document in Rochdale Observer, 3 June 1891
2. Rochdale Household Almanack. 1901
3. Manchester Guardian, 7 December 1842
4. Rochdale Observer, 3 October 1900 — interview with Abraham Greenwood.
5. G.D.H. Cole, op.cit., p.63
6. Rochdale Observer, 3 October 1900 op.cit.
7. Ibid.
8. Handbill, Rochdale Local Studies.
9. Rochdale Observer, 21 September 1861
10. Rochdale Spectator, August 1845
11. From G.D.H. Cole, op.cit., pp.402-411

Bibliography

1. Primary Sources

i Newspaper and Journals

Black Dwarf, 1820-1822
Courier, 1808, 1818-1820
Halifax Guardian, 1848-1850
Leeds Mercury, 1783
Manchester and Salford Advertiser, 1839, 1840-1842
Manchester Courier, 1840-1842
Manchester Mercury, 1830
Manchester Times & Examiner, 1828-1831
Northern Star, 1838-1846
People's Paper by Ikey, 1848
Rochdale Almanack, (Clegg's), 1870-1900
Rochdale Observer, 1856-1868
Rochdale Pilot, 1847-1848, 1863-1867
Rochdale Sentinel, 1853-1855
Rochdale Spectator, 1844-1847
Rochdale Standard, 1856-1857
Rochdale Times, 1870
The Times, 1808
United Trades Co-operative Journal, 1830
Newspaper cuttings books, Rochdale Libraries Local Studies Collection.

ii Commercial and Trades Directories

Pigot and Dean's Directory for Manchester and Salford, 1818, 1821, 1824
Wardle and Bentham's Directory for Manchester and District 1814-1815, 1816-1817

iii Poll Books and Electoral Registers

1832 (hand transcribed — Rochdale Libraries Local Studies Collection), 1835, 1841

iv Manuscript Material

Broadsheet Collection, Rochdale Libraries Local Studies Collection; particularly material relating to the Parliamentary election of 1832, political squibs produced in 1842 and items relating to the Rochdale Savings Bank.

Home Office Disturbance Papers, Public Record Office, Kew; particularly H.O. 40/37: Disturbances 1838 Lancashire, Rochdale: H.O. 41/17: Disturbances — Entry Book Provinces; H.O. 45/249: Correspondence from Captain of 11th Hussars at Rochdale to Lieutenant General Lord Fitzroy (26 August 1842) etc.

Plug Plot Riots, Depositions etc. Lancashire Record Office — QJD 1/157.Also material relating to conflict and disturbances at 1,5,8.

Poor Relief. Township administrative records (Hundersfield and Spotland), Rochdale Libraries Local Studies collection.

Rochdale Police Commissioners Minutes, Lancashire Record Office — CBR, particularly CRB1/1:1830-1839, CRB/1/2:1839-1844

Spotland Township Ratebook 1834, Rochdale Libraries Local Studies Collection.

Transcripts of Correspondence: John Bright to Duncan McLaren; Thomas Chadwick to Charles Chadwick, Rochdale Libraries Local Studies Collection; Thomas Chadwick to John Fielden, Rochdale Libraries Local Studies Collection.

Wadsworth Mss., John Rylands Library, Manchester.

v Government Publications etc.

British Parliamentary Papers

Report made by Mr. Tufnell or other Assistant Commissioners in October 1841 as to the State of the Poor in the Borough of Rochdale pp.1842 (89)xxxv, 171

Census of Great Britain 1851, Population Tables Vol. 1., Report 1852-3, LxxxV: Vol.II, LxxxVI

Census of England and Wales 1861, Population Tables; Numbers and Distribution of the People. Vol. 1, 1862, L1

Census population statistics 1801-1861

Select Committee on Combination Laws, 1825

2. Secondary Sources

i Contemporary Source Material

Baines, E., *History of the County Palatine and Duchy of Lancaster.* (J. Harland, ed.) Routledge, 1868
Baines, E., *Directory and Gazeteer of Lancashire.* 1825
Baines, T., *Lancashire and Cheshire Past and Present.* Mackenzie. 1868
Butterworth, J., *History of Rochdale and Saddleworth.* 1828
Ernest Jones: Who is he? Manchester. Pamphlet, Rochdale Libraries Local Studies Collection. No author, no date.
Fishwick, H., *History of the Parish of Rochdale.* author, Rochdale 1889
Fishwick, H., *Rochdale Jubilee.* Rochdale Corporation. 1906
Heape, C. and R., *Records of the Family of Heape.* Privately printed for author. 1906

Holyoake, G.J., *History of Co-operation.* Swan Sonnenschein, 1893

Labee, M., *Life and Times of Thomas Livsey.* Heywood. 1865

Mattley, R., *Annals of Rochdale.* Rochdale Times. 1899

Robertson, W., *Life and Times of John Bright.* author, Rochdale 1877

Robertson, W., *Old and New Rochdale.* author, Rochdale 1881

Robertson, W., Rochdale, the Home of Co-operation. in *Handbook of the 24 Annual Co-operative Conference* Co-operative Printing Union, 1892

Robertson, W., *Social and Political History of Rochdale.* author 1889

Rochdale Wills proved at Chester: Transcription by H. Brierley. Rochdale Libraries Local Studies Collection.

Royds, C.M., *The Pedigree of the Family of Royds.* author, 1910

Victoria County History of the Counties of England *A History of Lancashire Vol.V.* 1911

ii Books, pamphlets and journals

Briggs, A. (ed) *Chartist Studies.* MacMillan. 1963

Cole, G.D.H. *A Century of Co-operation.* George Allen and Unwin, 1944

Crossick, G. The Labour Aristocracy and its Values: A Study of Kentish London, *Victorian Studies.* Vol.XIX, No.3 (March 1976)

Epstein, J., *The Lion of Freedom.* Croom Helm. 1982

Epstein, J. and Thompson, D. *The Chartist Experience* : Studies in Working Class Radicalism and Culture, Methuen. 1982

Dutton, H.I. and King, J.E. *Ten Percent and No Surrender:* C.U.P. 1981

Foster, J., *Class Struggle and the Industrial Revolution.* Methuen 1977

Gadian, D.S., Class Consciousness in Oldham and other North-West Industrial Towns. *Historical Journal:* Vol.21, No.1 (1978)

Garrard, J., *Leadership and Power in Victorian Industrial Towns.* 1830-1880. M.U.P. 1983

Glenn, R., *Urban Workers in the Early Industrial Revolution.* Croom Helm 1984

Gray, R.Q., *The Aristocracy of Labour in Nineteenth Century Britain.* Methuen 1981

Gray, R.Q., *The Labour Aristocracy in Victorian Edinburgh.* Oxford, 1976

Hammond, J.L. and Hammond, B., *The Skilled Labourer.* Longman 1979

Harrison,R., *Before the Socialists.* Routledge and Kegan Paul 1965

Hinton, J., The Labour Aristocracy. *New Left Review* (32). 1965

Hobsbawm, E.J., *Labouring Men* Weidenfeld and Nicholson. 1964

Hobsbawm, E.J., *The Age of Revolution.* Abacus. 1977

Jones, G.S., Class Struggle and the Industrial Revolution. *New Left Review* (90). 1970

Jones, G.S., The Language of Chartism in Epstein, J. and Thompson,D. (eds). *The Chartist Experience.* Macmillan. 1982

Jones, G.S., *Languages of Class.* C.U.P. 1983

Kirk, N., *The Growth of Reformism in Mid-Victorian England.* Croom Helm 1985

Moorhouse, H.F.,The Marxist Theory of the Labour Aristocracy. *Social History.* Vol.3. No.1

Morris, R.J., *Class and Class Consciousness in the Industrial Revolution.* 1780-1850. Methuen. 1979

Musson, A.B., Class Struggle and the Labour Aristocracy, 1830-1860. *Social History.* (3) 1976

Penn, R., *Skilled Workers in the Class Structure.* C.U.P. 1985

Rose, A.G.,Truckling Magistrates of Lancashire in 1842. *Transaction of the Lancashire and Cheshire Antiquarian Society.* Vol.83. 1985

Rose, M.E., Rochdale Man and the Stalybridge Riots in Donajgrodski, A.P. (ed) *Social Control in the Nineteenth Century.* Croom Helm, 1975

Thompson, D., *The Chartists.* Temple Smith. 1984

Thompson, E.P., *The Making of the English Working Class.* Gollancz 1963

Turner, H.A., *Trade Union Growth and Policy.* George Allen and Union. 1962

Wadsworth, A.P., Early Factory System in the Rochdale District. *Transactions of the Rochdale Literary and Scientific Society.* xix. 136

Wadsworth, A.P., History of the Rochdale Woollen Trade. *Transactions of the Rochdale Literary and Scientific Society.* xv.90

Webb, S., and Webb. B., *History of Trades Unionism to 1920.* Longmans 1921